BEYOND GENRE

*New Directions
in Literary Classification*

BEYOND GENRE

New Directions in Literary Classification

PAUL HERNADI

Cornell University Press | ITHACA AND LONDON

First published 1972 by Cornell University Press.
Published in the United Kingdom by Cornell University Press Ltd., 2-4 Brook Street, London W1Y 1AA.

International Standard Book Number 0-8014-0732-X
Library of Congress Catalog Card Number 72-4175

Printed in the United States of America by Vail-Ballou Press, Inc.

Librarians: Library of Congress cataloging information appears on the the last page of the book.

Contents

Preface

Interest in genre has been growing among contemporary critics of various persuasions. About four years ago, for example, Poland's semiannual *Zagadnienia Rodzajów Literackich* (Problems of Literary Genres) found its American counterpart in the quarterly *Genre*. Yet most critics propounding new generic concepts or endorsing old ones show little awareness of the full theoretical horizon against which recent genre criticism operates. Indeed, no real effort seems to have been made to collect and interrelate the pertinent ideas of the last decades.

The three middle chapters of this book attempt to fill that curious gap in the literary self-awareness of our time. There is a sense, of course, in which the gap cannot be filled, for every instance of literary study contains, implies, or negates some consideration of genre. In surveying the vast field of twentieth-century criticism, I have tried to compensate for the unavoidable incompleteness by adopting a broadly based principle of selection: I have focused on classifications of the whole of literature and have discussed studies of individual genres only if I could see how they contribute to a better understanding of the entire realm of verbal art. As a result, the three chapters of the survey cover sixty or so modern theories that have, or in my view should have, influenced the climate of recent criticism as they have highlighted the merits or shortcomings of certain basic orientations.

To be sure, my "reduction" of some twenty thousand pages to about two hundred could have produced a critic's digest of rather dubious value. I have tried to escape that danger by reducing in the original sense of the word: by *leading* the discussed arguments *back* to their formative principles. In other words, I have presented the views of others with a fair amount of openly acknowledged commentary. Only in this way could I hope to do more than trace the present horizon of genre criticism, and I wanted to do more. As the reader will soon discover, my greater ambition has been to suggest how our critical vision might be sharpened.

The brunt of this task falls to the first chapter and, more particularly, to the last, where I have outlined a theory of literary classification that tries to avoid the customary pitfalls by assimilating much of the best contemporary thought about genre—and beyond. My conviction that genre concepts should be employed and transcended rather than ignored, codified, or rejected seems to be shared by many modern critics. Metaphorically speaking, the clay block of existing opinion seldom needed to be enlarged to yield my "Conclusions and Propositions." In some respects I have mainly done the potter's job of discarding what I considered excess material. Yet the same clay might have been used differently. My survey presents it for those wishing to shape it otherwise, perhaps to my greater satisfaction.

My personal interest in literary theory dates back to the early sixties, even though I was then finishing my first doctoral thesis in another field, the history of the theater, at the University of Vienna. I hardly need to say that the present book could not have been written had I not studied subsequently at Yale with René Wellek, a master historian of criticism, and Peter Demetz, my extremely helpful dissertation adviser. Yet I have incurred many other intellectual debts as well. Here I wish to express my gratitude to those friends, colleagues, and former professors of mine who offered their opinions after reading, or listening to, various versions of the arguments advanced in the following pages: Margret Dietrich, Iván Eröd, Oskar Holl, Robert Lichter, Kent McPherron, Elisabeth Stengel, and István Zelenka in Vienna; Cyrus Hamlin, A. M. Nagler, Lowry Nelson, Jr., and Steven Scher in New Haven, Connecticut; Dirk Baay, Timothy Fuller, Carlton Gamer, J. Glenn Gray, and Herving Madruga in Colorado Springs; Philip Berk, Peter Dunn, Alfred Geier, Alfred Kuhn, Kurt Weinberg, and Eléonore Zimmermann in Rochester, New York.

I am indebted to the National Council of Teachers of English and to the editor of *Comparative Literature* for their permission to reprint extensively from my articles published in *College English* and *Comparative Literature*. Further acknowledgments are due to Colorado College for a 1968 summer research grant and to the University of Rochester for congenial teaching assignments and for secretarial help since 1969. Last but not least, I should mention that the staff of Cornell University Press has contributed much care and expertise to the finished product, which I wish to dedicate to my critics within the family, Miklós and Virginia.

PAUL HERNADI

Rochester, New York

BEYOND GENRE

*New Directions
in Literary Classification*

Chapter One

The Genres of Genre Criticism

Few concepts of literary criticism are quite as "literary" as the concept of genre. Works by the same author and those written in the same language or the same period make up distinct groups, yet the critic's interest in such groups tends to widen and to blur the literary perspective. The study of genres is different: it may profit from the advance of knowledge in such related fields as psychology, linguistics, or sociology without softening its focus on the works of literature. Small wonder that the idea of literary kinds has attracted the majority of critics ever since Socrates in the third book of Plato's *Republic* distinguished three modes of poetic discourse. Being less incidental than critiques of individual works but more concrete than philosophical theories of literature as a whole, discriminating concepts of genre can provide something like mortar for the edifice of literary criticism. After all, knowing what kinds of literature have been possible means knowing a great deal about literature as well.

Yet there is a price to pay for such knowledge: the prevailing generic concepts of a period often form the literary horizon beyond which no contemporary reader is likely to see. This is why constant testing of one's conceptual framework is needed from new and ever-changing perspectives. As Friedrich Schlegel's 53rd *Athenaeum-Fragment* reminds us:

"It is equally lethal for the mind to have a system and to have none. It will very well have to decide to combine the two."

Having a system, yet knowing that it is one among many possible systems, may be the best response to the challenge of Schlegel's paradox. Such an open-minded attitude particularly fits the student of genre concepts as he faces a large variety of "systems" and the concomitant conflict between the theoretical and historical aspects of his inquiry. On the one hand, concepts of drama or tragedy make us see literature as a synchronic order of coexisting works; such concepts stress the similarity between *Oedipus the King* and *Macbeth* at the expense of the historical differences between them. On the other hand, the diachronic sequence in which literary works are read and interpreted has considerable impact on genre concepts: our conscious or unformulated idea of tragedy partly relies on the nature of our acquaintance with *Oedipus the King*, yet our understanding of that play partly relies on the idea of tragedy we have derived from our previous literary experience. Thus "theory" and "history" permanently interact in every reader's mind, and this interaction presents Günther Müller's remarkable quandary (p. 136) to the critic interested in literary classification: How can I define tragedy (or any other genre) before I know on which works to base the definition, yet how can I know on which works to base the definition before I have defined tragedy?

This pair of questions was persuasively related by Karl Viëtor (p. 441) to the central dilemma of hermeneutics: how can we fully understand individual parts of a text before the whole text has been fully understood and *vice versa?* Indeed, the genre critic can only solve his problem by entering a version of that not so vicious Circle of Hermeneutics. While considering *Hamlet*, for example, he must shift his attention back and forth between this specific "part" and the operative "whole" of his literary experience. In so doing, he will discover resemblances between *Hamlet* and other works of literature, but he will not rigidly impose a generic concept emerging from his previous literary experience on the work under present study. Instead of permitting preconceived generic expectations to distort his response to the work, he will stay ready to revise his idea of a genre in the light of new experience. Such flexibility in deciding what "kind" of work we are considering is indeed essential. As Eric Donald Hirsch ably argued in his *Validity in Interpretation* (1967), our very understanding of a text is influenced by the "last, unrevised generic concept" we apply to it (p. 77).

So much for the individual reader or critic. Yet there is another, less private type of interplay between the synchronic and diachronic aspects of genre criticism. Literary works are not only read but also written one after another. In a sense, therefore, the diachronic sequence of history determines how much and what kind of theoretical insight is potentially available in a given decade or century. This means that even an "omniscient" reader—Diderot's enlightened fantasy of the ideal critic, for example—would have to be familiar with the entire body of literature at a particular moment of its history; he could not avoid "knowing" individual works as they merge into one, and not another, synchronic pattern. As Molière's contemporary, the Ideal Critic would applaud or reject the Misanthrope as a comic figure; as Rousseau's, he could hardly help but see him as the unduly ridiculed hero of a "tearful comedy"; as Goethe's, he might even decide to regard him as tragic; and as ours, he would probably align

Alceste with such tragicomic misanthropes as Shakespeare's Timon, Lessing's Tellheim, and Ionesco's Bérenger in *Rhinoceros*.

Whoever wants to deal with the genre of Molière's play undogmatically will not ignore such historically conditioned reinterpretations of its main character. Rather, he will grant that criticism by genres has very little in common with the botanist's or the zoologist's unequivocal classification of species. Indeed, Charles E. Whitmore (1924), Irwin Ehrenpreis (1945), Eliseo Vivas (1968), Claudio Guillén (1970), and other critics have suggested or implied that the framing or endorsing of a genre concept *need not* mean more than this: we have discerned some similarity between certain works. Of course, such a loose way of defining genre might lead to extreme relativism. One could argue, for instance, that all works of literature are similar to each other in many ways and that it depends entirely on the critic's point of view which similarities he should consider important enough for generic distinctions. One could further claim that the philosopher Karl R. Popper has forcibly defended a relativistic concept of similarity. According to a persuasive appendix in Popper's *Logic of Scientific Discovery* (1959), "things may be similar in *different respects*," and "any two things which are from one point of view similar may be dissimilar from another point of view." On the basis of these observations Popper suggests that any group of things will display some similarity if, "with a little ingenuity," we select an appropriate point of view from which to consider the group (pp. 421f). If we apply this conclusion to literary works, we shall see why it has often been less difficult to devise a possible system of generic classification than to avoid useless ones. But Popper's concept of similarity cannot fully explain why a rather small number of basic genre concepts have prevailed, with important modifications to be sure, throughout the recorded history of literary criticism. The reason for the frequent recurrence of certain concepts is, of course, that the serious critic's point of view is to some extent shared by many of his colleagues who will join him in considering some similarities between given works more significant than others. This fact corroborates a fundamental principle of *gestalt* theory exemplified by the diagrams appearing on pp. 200 and 210 of the first edition (1929) of Wolfgang Köhler's *Gestalt Psychology*.*

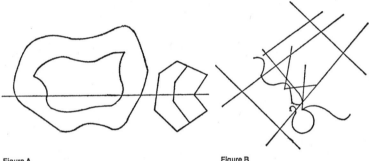

Figure A   Figure B

Few persons will spontaneously notice the presence of the numerical sign 4 as an aspect of similarity between the two figures. While Figure B naturally gives away sign 4 as one of its outstanding features, the pattern of Figure A "hides" the same digit until we abstract the lines making up a 4 in the approximate center of the diagram from adjoining parts of the three more conspicuous units of the design. Although the lines making up a 4 act upon our retina in both Figure A and Figure B, we are likely to perceive it while viewing one

* From *Gestalt Psychology* by Wolfgang Köhler. Permission of Liveright, Publisher, New York. Copyright ® 1956 by Liveright Publishing Corporation.

pattern but not while viewing the other. The moral is simple enough: Figure B does, Figure A does not, invite us to select a point of view from which the digit 4 becomes salient in the respective designs.

The issues involved in genre criticism are more complex than our drawings might suggest. Yet the critic confronting those issues can learn a good deal from Popper's and Köhler's arguments. Heeding Popper's advice, he will realize that the inevitable choice of a point of view makes him aware of a particular set of similarities between works of literature. Mindful of Köhler's insights, however, he will trust that his esthetic sensitivity prescribes a point of view from which significant similarities become noticeable. As a result, the critic will not claim universal validity for his generic concepts. Yet he will assume that concepts promoting his understanding of literature rely on salient aspects in the *gestalt* of literary works. Fully aware of the fact that no concept of genre is self-evident, he will further recognize the importance of clarifying which similarities he is particularly interested in and why.

With the last point in mind, it seems useful to distinguish four main types of similarity as possible bases for theories of genre. Some critics discuss the similarity between the mental attitudes of authors as responsible for the similarity between literary works. Others stress the similar effect some works are likely to have on a reader's mind. Yet works of literature are verbal evocations of imaginative worlds rather than simple vehicles of communication between writer and reader. Thus two other types of similarity deserve more careful attention. These are the similarity between literary works considered as verbal constructs and the similarity between the imaginative worlds different verbal constructs evoke. Slightly modifying a set of distinctions Meyer H. Abrams has suggested in *The Mirror and the Lamp* (1953), we can attribute a given critic's primary concern with the author, the reader, the verbal medium, or the evoked world to his predominantly "expressive," "pragmatic," "structural," or "mimetic" orientation. Extreme adherence to any of the four basic approaches will lead to one of four familiar pitfalls of criticism: the Intentional Fallacy, the Affective Fallacy,[1] dogmatic formalism, or preoccupation with "message" and subject matter. But tactful critics can focus on any kind of generic similarity without losing sight of the limitations inherent in their preferred approach.

Lesser minds, of course, kept devising rigid and one-sided generic systems, and men like Giordano Bruno or Johann Gottfried Herder were bound to reject those systems as the subduing of genius to the yoke of rules. At the turn of our century, similar disenchantment prompted Benedetto Croce to swear to wage his "eternal war against the disastrous division of literature" into genres. To be sure, modern critics have continued to explore generic similarities. Yet, perhaps under Croce's indirect influence, they tend to realize that the study of genres must not become an end in itself but rather serve as a means toward the fuller understanding of individual works and of literature as a whole. Indeed, the most stimulating trends in recent genre criticism point beyond any literal concept of genre by avoiding three objectionable traits of many previous theories. Instead of pigeonholing the apparent average and censuring the manifestly exceptional, the best twentieth-century critics look for partial resemblances be-

[1] I adopt these vivid terms from the titles of two essays by W. K. Wimsatt and M. C. Beardsley without subscribing to the entire arguments presented there. Cf. William K. Wimsatt, *The Verbal Icon.*

tween unique individuals. Instead of setting up firm boundaries between different kinds of literature, they present the results of generic observations as "ideal types"—Max Weber's influential term for conceptual models—to which literary works correspond in varying degree. Instead of tracing sources and modifications within narrow generic traditions, they act on the premise that the study of historical change could greatly profit from a clearer view than we now have of what is changing. The better part of recent genre criticism has thus tended to be descriptive rather than prescriptive, tentative rather than dogmatic, and philosophical rather than historical. In this last respect, many modern critics seem to share the opinion Claude Lévi-Strauss has expressed in another context: "Darwin would not have been possible if he had not been preceded by Linnaeus, that is to say, if one had not already laid the theoretical and methodological bases permitting to describe and define the species which are subject to change" (p. 41).

The new or newly rediscovered avenues of literary classification lead beyond the conceptual sphere of genre in any but the widest sense of the word. Indeed, a large number of modern critics have felt induced to reconsider the very axioms of the genre approach. This unprejudiced attitude, coupled with considerable theoretical penetration, could have resulted in deeper insights into the "kinds" as well as the whole of literature, had differences in taste and tradition not prevented most twentieth-century critics from sincerely probing each other's opinions. Yet such probing is needed if we want to do more than just complain that terminological confusion keeps the various critical approaches of our day from becoming effectively integrated. Granted, it may not be possible or even desirable to reunify the languages spoken in a perfect Babel. What I try to do in the next three chapters is to provide something like a multilingual dictionary for fellow Babelites so that each of us can better understand what the others have to say, should we choose to listen.

To conclude these introductory remarks (and to anticipate the evaluative criteria of the survey) I want to state four principles which have guided my own thinking about genre and beyond. They will fully emerge, I hope, from my Conclusions and Propositions. In that last chapter of the book I am outlining a theory of literature which intends, first, to account for noteworthy similarities between literary works in a way that promotes the understanding of literature at large; second, to provide adaptable concepts for the comparative discussion of individual works, not ready-made labels for their instant classification; third, to approach works of literature as verbal evocations of imaginative worlds; and fourth, to discuss the modes of literary evocation and its results in two different but related conceptual frameworks, both of which make us see literature as verbal art presenting and representing human action and vision.

Chapter Two

The Writer and the Reader

1. *Expressive Concepts*

The critics to be discussed in the first part of this chapter approach literary works primarily as products of articulated self-expression. Emphasizing the relation between the written page and the man who wrote it, they ascribe similarities between works by different authors to similarities between the minds of these authors. Since Benedetto Croce's *Estetica* (1902) rejects genre criticism on very "expressive" premises indeed, it seems appropriate to recall his main argument as our point of departure.

In a rather original epistemological system Croce distinguishes two kinds of knowledge: the intuitive (brought forth in language and the arts by the expression of impressions) and the conceptual (attained through philosophical and scientific inquiry). His central objection to the division of art into arts and the arts into genres is based on that postulated dichotomy. Croce discards all such categories of literary criticism as "tragic," "comic," "epic," or "dramatic" action, "domestic life," "chivalry," or "idyll," simply because they are not impressions whose expression might constitute the "esthetic fact," but universal and abstract concepts; not "contents" to be formed intuitively by esthetic expression, but "forms" resulting from logical expression. Since, for

Croce, "the logical or scientific form as such excludes the esthetic form," he feels justified in concluding: "He who begins to think scientifically has already ceased to contemplate esthetically" (p. 36).

Beyond doubt, the last statement grossly generalizes about a subject which is far from being empirically explored. Yet the validity of Croce's conclusion need not be disputed here. Even if it should be impossible for the critic to perceive on an esthetic plane and to reflect in conceptual terms simultaneously, there is no reason why he could not alternate between these two kinds of mental activity while performing his office. Thus he may very well frame generic concepts which reflect his response to a given group of "esthetic expressions."

No similarity between literary works *as we know them* can, of course, mitigate Croce's resolute aversion toward genre. To him "form" means the first intuitive expression of impressions—the supposedly fully fledged idea of a work —in the artist's mind. Consequently, Croce's *Esthetics* must dismiss the actual appearance of art works as a mere "translation of the esthetic fact into physical phenomena (sounds, tones, movements, combinations of lines and colors)" (pp. 96f). Indeed, most of Croce's practical criticism focuses on the "leading sentiment" of authors, that is to say, on the substance which a writer's esthetic expressions disclose most successfully. Croce ignores the fact that even this limited view of the critic's function and competence entails the possibility of generic distinctions. For the majority of expressive critics, any similarity between mental attitudes supposed to have been present in different writers' minds provides clues for the classification of literary works.

The first large-scale attempt to challenge Croce on his

own ground was undertaken in Ernest Bovet's decidedly expressive treatment of *Lyrisme épopée, drame* (1911). In fact, the polemical appendix "M. Benedetto Croce et les genres littéraires" reads today as the most suggestive section of Bovet's somewhat puzzling *opus*. Bovet realizes that Croce's firm rejection of generic categories must be seen (and to some extent welcomed) as a reaction to the excessive positivism and historicism of the preceding generation. He also seems right in assuming that Ferdinand Brunetière's pseudobiological *L'Évolution des genres* (1890) "exasperated" Croce simply because the two critics were "diametrically opposed minds"—a "law-maker" and a "poet of individual creation" (pp. 250f). Convincingly enough, Bovet argues that both the positivists (who observe similarities between isolated elements of different works) and Croce (who insists on the uniqueness of every work of art) are partially justified; it is mainly due to their differing methods, analysis *versus* synthesis, that they must come to disparate conclusions. "But why should we not, with all reservations that prudence demands, combine analysis and synthesis by discerning the common elements on the one hand and the individual combinations on the other?" (p. 245). This interrogative suggestion is sound even though it needs supplementing: not only the "elements" of individual combinations but also the ways in which elements are combined may be similar.

Bovet's actual theory is far less penetrating than his methodological considerations. He assumes that the division of literature into the lyric, the epic, and the dramatic genre has been a *consensus omnium* in all times and relates each of these generic categories to one of three "essential modes of conceiving life and the universe." The lyric emerges between the extreme poles of faith and despair; the epic encompasses action and passion; drama charts a crisis tending toward serenity. The three modes represent the characteristic vision of youth (lyric), maturity (epic), and old age (drama), but it is possible for the same person to incline toward one shortly after the other or, in exceptional cases, even at the same time. There are innumerable transitions between the three types; in all literary works, however, we can find one prevailing mode of seeing the world, and everything else in the work is subordinated to this dominant mode of vision (pp. 13ff).

Bovet's treatment of literary genres as suggestive of youth, maturity, or old age closely follows Victor Hugo's comments on lyric, epic, and dramatic literature and their respective prototypes—the Old Testament, Homer, and Shakespeare. Indeed, Bovet proposes to elaborate on the "fundamental truth" of Hugo's celebrated Preface to *Cromwell* (1827) without duplicating Hugo's errors concerning details. But what he really does is to push Hugo's fanciful analogy between the "three ages" of mankind and of individual nations and the three types of literature to absurd extremes. In all seriousness Bovet declares that youth, maturity, and old age characterize three periods in all historical eras, each of which is in turn "dominated by one great political, moral, or social principle" (pp. 32, 214). Each first or lyric period welcomes the emerging principle as a new and definitive faith; the epic vision of second periods corresponds to the realization of the principle; and the third or dramatic period of every era witnesses the crisis and disintegration of the old principle as well as the germination of a new one (p. 17). That such a dogmatic method of periodization must blur the literary perspective becomes especially obvious in the case of the "second era" of French literature, the age of absolute monarchy, which Bovet divides into three "periods": 1520–1610, 1610–1715, 1715–1789. Although the dates are given as approximations, they compel Bovet to interpret Rabelais as a primarily lyric poet, and to explain the presence of Corneille, Racine, and Molière in a fundamentally "epic" period. Clearly, there is a price to pay for discovering what Bovet's subtitle announces as *Une loi de l'histoire littéraire expliquée par l'évolution générale.*

In *Das Formgesetz der epischen, dramatischen und lyrischen Dichtung* (1923), Ernst Hirt set out to establish not a "law of literary history" but the "law of form" underlying narrative, dramatic, and lyric literature. In delineating his predominantly expressive theory, Hirt adapts two structural concepts, "representation" and "report," to the familiar distinction of German romantic philosophers between the self (*Ich*) and the world: the subject "represents itself," of objects we obtain "reports." Drama and lyric poetry consist exclusively of representation, that is, the self-representation (*Selbstdarstellung*) of the dramatic characters or of the poet. The epic alternates between the narrator's report about the characters, his self-representation (contemplating, evaluating passages), and the self-representation of the fictional figures (dialogue). Hirt argues that the three genres correspond to three situations in which a writer may find himself with regard to the "world-process" (*Allgeschehen*): he may either view it from without (epic) or experience it from within, and in the latter case he will either experience it as an individual (lyric) or, through identification, from the experiential standpoint of several individuals (drama). Metaphorically speaking, the lyric poet is one wave in the current of progressing time; the dramatic poet permeates all the waves; the epic poet stands on the riverside and describes what he sees (pp. 7ff).

Hirt's metaphors surely approximate the impressions of a reader who would stop and wonder about the relationship between the "contents" and "the author's voice" in a song, a play, or a novel. There is a good deal of affinity between the monologue form and self-representation, between the dialogue form and the simultaneous representation of several "selves," and between the combination of report, monologue, and dialogue and the shifting distance of the storyteller's vantage point from the narrated events. But Hirt goes too far when he identifies the lyric and epic "I" with the author, or when he declares that playwrights experience life "in the rhythm of struggle" (pp. 83f).

Further advances in the same direction were to follow as the somewhat loose notion of "worldview" (*Weltanschauung*) induced several critics publishing in German between the two World Wars to move away from the literary basis of generic distinctions. Unlike Hirt, many of these writers seem to have approached literature mainly to find suitable illustrations for ingenious systems of speculative anthropology. In an almost purely philosophical argument modifying Wilhelm Dilthey's *Weltanschauungstypen*, Max Wundt, for example, has aligned epic, lyric, and dramatic poetry with a naturalistic, a psychologistic, and an idealistic worldview, respectively (pp. 415ff).

In his *Präludium zur Poesie* (1929), Theophil Spoerri suggested a similarly grandiose but more thought-provoking set of generic correspondences: the "static" worldview of the epic poet is focused on exterior things in their own context; the "dynamic" lyric is animated by the inner energy of the soul; and drama embodies the "directive norms" of the spirit. It follows (and why shouldn't it?) that the epic poet conceives of reality as world, body, thing, common sense, and the past; the aspects of the lyric worldview are: I, soul, impulse, emotion, and the present; and drama points to the realm of norms: God, spirit or mind (*Geist*), value, will, and the future. There are many combinations and transitions, but as we move from epic through lyric toward drama the tension increases both in the vision that prevails and in the form of language that is adequate to it: prose, verse, and the "explosive power and packed fullness" of dialogue (pp. 148f, 322).

In his book on *Die literarische Wertung* (1938), Leonhard Beriger singled out more specific ideological premises for a number of more concretely defined literary genres. "Great lyric poetry" (such as Goethe's, Hölderlin's, Mörike's, Shelley's, and Keats's) emerges from a mystic-pantheistic *Weltgefühl;* tragedy from a dualistic-idealistic *Weltbild;* the novel from determinism and skepticism; and the *Novellen* of the Italian Renaissance and German Romanticism from the "belief in the significance of an individual's fate" (pp. 93ff).

Robert Petsch, whose voluminous critical work abounds in insight as well as commonplace, devoted separate books to the literary manifestations of "the epic man" (*Wesen und Formen der Erzählkunst*, 1934), "the lyric man" (*Die lyrische Dichtkunst—Ihr Wesen und Formen*, 1939), and "the dramatic man" (*Wesen und Formen des Dramas*, 1945). Petsch's lengthy discussions of the basic mental attitudes underlying narrative, lyric, and dramatic literature liberally draw on generic concepts propounded in Germany between about 1800 and 1830: Goethe's and Schiller's archetypes of epic and dramatic literature (detached rhapsodist versus involved actor); A. W. Schlegel's and Hegel's view of drama as a synthesis of the subjective lyric and the objective epic; and, above all, Goethe's distinction between the three "natural forms of poetry" (the lyric mode of enthusiastic excitement, the epic mode of lucid narration, and the dramatic mode of personal action). No doubt all these concepts deserve careful reinterpretation. But Petsch's wax cabinet of the enthusiastically singing, contemplatively narrating, and dynamically acting "men" yields lifeless abstractions rather than helpful generalizations about the result of writing poems, novels, or plays.

For the most part, Spoerri's, Beriger's, and Petsch's generic speculations fail to transcend certain narrow areas of literary history. Their concept of lyric poetry, for instance, encompasses little more than the lyric poetry of Romanticism, or perhaps only the songlike poems of Goethe and the German romanticists. Since, however, it would be unwarranted to impute Beriger's mystic-pantheistic worldview to Horace, to look for Petsch's singer in Donne, or to demand Spoerri's dynamism from Petrarca and T. S. Eliot, we may even wonder whether the lyric masterpieces of German Romanticism really reflect, from the point of view of their *genre*, the poets' supposed *Weltanschauung*.

Another brand of expressive criticism attempts to establish connections between a writer's preferred genre and the structure of his psyche. In his *Versuch einer psychologischen Grundlegung der Dichtungsgattungen* (1924), Robert Hartl distinguished three psychological types of "world-experience" (*Welterleben*) as constitutive of three types of literature. In the last analysis, Hartl's concepts of the epic, the lyric, and the dramatic genre correspond to Immanuel Kant's three "faculties of the soul" (*Seelenvermögen*): thinking, feeling, and volition. At the same time, however, Hartl attempts to spell out his recourse to speculative anthropology in the more empirical terms of early twentieth-century psychology. Accepting Adolf Stöhr's description of the different functions of the nervous system, Hartl connects drama with "motoric experience" (experience related to purposive motion), narrative fiction with "imaginative experience" (the contemplating employment of the imagination), lyric poetry with "vasomotoric" (that is: emotional) experience.

Rather than dwell on what he thinks is an obvious relationship between feeling and lyric poetry, Hartl devotes his attention to the difference between *Epik* and *Dramatik*. Most important of all, he gives a radically "expressive" turn to Goethe's, Jean Paul Richter's, and Hegel's association of narrative literature with occurrence (*Begebenheit*) and drama with action (*Taten, Handlung*). He argues that, since epic as well as dramatic works concern themselves with events that take place between human beings and inside human minds, it depends on the "experiential disposition" of a writer whether he regards those events as mere occurrences or as purposeful actions. In the first case he is predisposed to be an epic poet; in the second, a playwright. Whereas the epic poet's only "passion" is to contemplate in a detached manner what goes on within and without, the dramatist "wills, acts, and struggles" with every human being (p. 68). With "epic calmness" and a bent toward sensuous plasticity, the narrative writer strives to encompass the "extensive totality" of the world and the microcosmic "intensive totality" of his characters. In contrast, the playwright concentrates on one isolated purposeful action and, consequently, on the will of the *dramatis personae;* whatever is not connected with the volition of the figures has no "dramatic value" and has to be omitted from genuine drama. This concentration on the volitive elements compels the spectators to identify themselves with the purpose of the characters to the point of experiencing their impulses. Hence results the "motoric" effect, which is brought about by the playwright's dramatic disposition to conceive of his subject matter, and by his use of stichomythia and other devices characteristic of dramatic style (pp. 48, 70, *et passim*).

A considerable portion of Kenneth Burke's *Attitudes toward History* (1937) deals with literary genres in the light of Burke's private system of mental behavior—a highly undogmatic blend of (mainly Marxist) sociology and (mainly Freudian) depth psychology. Burke considers "Yes, No, and the intermediate realm of Maybe" as the basic attitudes in forming and reforming human congregations; and the "expressive forms" of literary genres represent for him "various typical ways in which these attitudes are both subtly and grandly symbolized" (p. 1). Not specifying whether his primary concern is with the writer's or the reader's attitude, Burke seems to assume that the same type of attitude more distinctly characterizes the author than the congenial reader of works belonging to a given genre.

Burke suggests that the great epic poem, tragedy, comedy, a genre termed humor, and the *carpe diem* type of lyric poetry provide "frames of acceptance." The *epic poem* makes humility and self-glorification "work together" by magnifying the character of the warlike hero to the size of the situation he confronts; contemplating the hero's deeds, one adopts a realistic sense of one's own limitations but also obtains, through partial identification with the great figure, the "distinction necessary for the needs of self-justification." *Humor* promotes acceptance the other way round; it is "dwarfing the situation" with an "attitude of 'happy stupidity'" whereby the gravity of life simply fails to register." *Tragedy* and *comedy* are allied in their repudiation of pride, yet tragedy exalts *hubris* as the root of awe-inspiring crimes while comedy dismisses it as a laughable mistake. In spite of this difference, both genres represent frames of acceptance advocating the advantage of the average person's limitations (pp. 37ff).

As far as the epic, humor, and comedy are concerned, Burke's argument is plausible. The greater part of his treatment of tragedy seems to me far less convincing. Burke suggests that "the rise of business individualism" in Periclean Athens "sharpened the awareness of personal ambition as a motive in human acts" and ascribes to the three great tragedians a "pious, orthodox, conservative, 'reactionary' attitude" toward this kind of *hubris* (p. 39). But it is clear that in Greek tragedy the *hubris* of heroic rulers, never that of merchants, was at stake. Thus if one wants to find a psychosociological motivation for what Burke rightly describes as tragedy's sympathetic dealing with crime, the ambivalent nostalgia of a democratic society for the heroic grandeur of the past seems to be more to the point than is Burke's interpretation.

Aware that the acceptance of *A* involves the rejection of *non-A*, Burke does not contrast acceptance and rejection as mutually exclusive (p. 57). It is, therefore, in a dialectically qualified sense that elegy, satire, and burlesque "reject." *Elegy* does so by a reversal of the strategy of humor: "It spreads the disproportion between the weakness of the self and the magnitude of the situation." But there is also an element of acceptance in elegy, for a person with a perfected technique of complaint will not shun situations enabling him to use such an equipment. Elegy seeks to develop tolerance to blows of great misfortune by stylistically administering misfortune in small doses; this "homeopathic" strategy, however, is not the best in situations where the danger could be eliminated otherwise. *Satire* attacks in others the weaknesses and temptations that trouble the satirist himself; it is "an approach *from without* to something *from within*." In *burlesque* and its related forms (polemic, caricature), there is no attempt to get inside the victim's psyche, and the biased selection of externals of behavior reaches its "logical conclusion" with the target's "reduction to absurdity" (pp. 44ff).

Although it is never clearly explained why the *grotesque* and the *didactic* belong to the "intermediate realm of Maybe," Burke seems to consider them as manifestations of that third type of attitude. Since he avowedly views his genres as "recordings on the dial," we need not blame him for the tendency of interpreting the indicators in other than literary terms. Yet in his various discussions of the grotesque (suggestively described as "the cult of incongruity *without* the laughter") and the didactic ("today usually called propaganda"), sociological interest prevails to the point of making doubtful whether Burke considers those two "preponderantly transitional" genres as genres of imaginative literature at all (pp. 57f).

What distinguishes Pierre Kohler's "Contribution à une philosophie des genres" (1938) and Paul Van Tieghem's concise "La Question des genres littéraires" (1938) from all "expressive" pronouncements discussed so far is the two critics' realization that the literary genres are, or at least can be, helpful guides to writers as conventional frames. Pierre Kohler regards artistic creation as a process of "ordering" (*mise en ordre*) that starts with selection and leads to construction. The idea of a genre stimulates and guides the artist in both creative phases. In the selective phase, generic conventions reduce the number of possibilities and thus promote the choice of elements that promise to enter into successful combinations. But the "rules" also support the writer's constructive work as they transmit whatever can be transmitted in a "usable formula" from the artistic achievements of the past. It is, therefore, through generic conventions that the principle of external and collective order can best interact with the poet's inborn temperament—his internal individual order. Kohler is even ready to defend rigid formal rules (like those of the *tragédie classique*) as required by the "profound need of the human soul" to express itself beautifully with the greatest force and smallest expenditure possible. In keeping with this monetary metaphor, Kohler suggests that "the genres are the economy of the arts and letters" (I, 235, 242; II, 137, 139).

Paul Van Tieghem revives the spirit of Hippolyte Taine's causal approach to literary history when he considers genres as the esthetic expressions of man's sentimental, intellectual, religious, or social needs and interests. According to Van Tieghem, every genre is a "mold" first designed by invention, then adapted and perfected by experience, to serve a definite purpose: once a genre becomes part of a literary tradition, one associates with it certain subject matters as well as certain patterns of thought and sentiment. The "true artist" will take full advantage of the tested and perfected "molds" by broadening or simplifying, modifying and "rejuvenating" them. Yet the adopted frame exerts a powerful influence on the writer's self-expression. To a considerable extent, the generic matrix determines the use which an author can make of his resources of imagination and observation; it will also more than suggest a specific degree of concentration or ramification of the plot as well as the relative importance of the characters and their milieu in the new work belonging to an established genre. Thus the choice of genre not only indicates psychological affinities but also defines which area of a writer's psyche may manifest itself in a given work (I, 97ff).

Invited by *The Times Literary Supplement* to set forth his critical credo, Emil Staiger deftly stated the task of literary study: "We must grasp what grips us." Since Staiger assumes that a writer's attitude toward the world leaves an unmistakable stamp on each of his esthetically successful works, he wants to "grasp what grips us" by recognizing and describing the literary manifestation of such attitudes—the style of a work, of an author, or that of an age. Accordingly, Staiger discusses the lyric, epic, and dramatic *styles*, not the lyric, epic, and dramatic *genres*, as "basic concepts" or *Grundbegriffe der Poetik* (1946). He observes that, although our terminology is already dominated by utter confusion, new works still induce critics to establish new divisions of literature. In order to overcome this predicament, Staiger suggests that we replace our concern for pigeonholing works into genres by an effort to explore the meaning of the descriptive terms "lyric," "epic," and "dramatic." All works belonging to one of the various subdivisions of lyric, epic, and dramatic literature should be considered as more or less consistent realizations of the ideas expressed by the triad of adjectives. Indeed, a generic category like "lyric drama" need not present the dilemma of a *contradictio in adiecto*, because the two words of the designation refer to different aspects of the works in question: the noun indicates their dialogue form, whereas the adjective describes their "key" (*Tonart*) in the musical sense of the word. In Staiger's opinion, criticism should concentrate on the nature of the "keys"—*das Lyrische, das Epische,* and *das Dramatische*—not on the stylistically less relevant "genres" *Lyrik, Epik,* and *Dramatik* (pp. 7f, 223ff). Clearly distinguishing the three adjectives from the three nouns, Staiger avoids what Günther Müller censured as "indiscriminate conceptual mixtures" involving the generic terms as such and their homonyms for different styles or moods. (Cf. "Bermerkungen zur Gattungspoetik," 1928, p. 147.)

Without disputing that we can find the closest approximations of the lyric style in poetry that is traditionally called lyric, Staiger insists that the concepts *lyrisch* and *Lyrik* are far from being identical. First, the different kinds of lyric poetry are *lyric* in various degrees: odes are "more" lyric than epigrams and "less" lyric than songs. Next, it is possible to grasp the "ideal significance" of the three styles (but not that of the "genres") outside of literary experience: a landscape may imprint on a mind the idea of "the lyric"; marching refugees, that of "the epic"; an altercation, that of "the dramatic." Finally, the relationship of the adjectives *lyrisch* or *dramatisch* to the nouns *Lyrik* or *Dramatik* corresponds to the relationship of *menschlich* to *Mensch* rather than to that of *hölzern* to *Holz.* Wood is wooden by definition, but not every man is humane and not every drama is primarily dramatic. The words "humane" and "dramatic" express ideas by which a man or a drama may, but need not, be substantially informed (pp. 9f, 236f, 239).

Staiger devotes the longest exploration to the lyric which he seems to consider the innermost shrine in the temple of literature. The lyric style emanates, as it were, from the inspired poet as long as the conformity between that which exists (*das Seiende*) and the poet prevails. There is no gap between subject and object; the poet's soul moves in a fluid element of moods and, in an act of inward-turning remembrance (*Erinnerung*), assimilates past, present, and future to its own nature. But the lyric "liquefaction of everything solid" can never become complete in the realm of literature where, by dint of the complex nature of language, the principles of the epic and the dramatic also operate. In turn, the presence of the lyric in all literature makes every literary work transcend the limits of rationality (pp. 61f, 70, 81).

The songs of Goethe and the German romanticists eminently partake, in Plato's sense of *metéchein*, of the nature of the lyric. The recurrence of sounds, rhythms, or even words and phrases secures the unity of mood in many of these poems. Some masterpieces, however, are short enough to dispense with refrains and elaborate rhyme schemes or rhythmical patterns. In poems like Goethe's "Über allen Gipfeln" [1] a lyric ideal, the complete interpenetration of sound and meaning, has been realized: a unique verbal pattern incarnates a unique poetic mood. The great significance of the sound stratum of language in lyric poetry induces Staiger to conclude that the lyric, if it could exist in an unmixed state, would be singing rather than talking. Even the literary (and hence impure) manifestations of the lyric avoid the logic of higher syntax; the lyric style tends to evolve in paratactical succession of loosely organized sentences. Hypotaxis and especially causal or final conjunctions and clauses quickly destroy the songlike atmosphere; "singing and thinking are incompatible" (pp. 16, 37, 241). The effect of small rear-

[1] See below, pp. 172f.

rangements (pp. 37f) in the first stanza of a poem by the playwright Friedrich Hebbel massively supports Staiger's argument:

Hebbel's "Lied"

Komm, wir wollen Erdbeern pflücken,
Ist es doch nicht weit zum Wald,
Wollen junge Rosen brechen,
Sie verwelken ja so bald!

Staiger's version.[2]

Wir wollen Erdbeern pflücken,
Es ist nicht weit zum Wald,
Und junge Rosen brechen,
Rosen verwelken so bald.

What has Staiger done? He has removed all words which overstress the situation (*komm, doch,* the second *wollen,* and *ja*) and repeated the word *Rosen* (instead of referring to the flowers by a colorless pronoun); he has also loosened the stubbornly trochaic pattern of Hebbel's verse. Such a simple operation has managed to turn the original lines into a stanza that approaches Staiger's ideal of the lyric style. Yet Staiger overlooks that the experimental manufacture of a sample blunts the metaphysical edge of his argument. With regard to the modified text (which can serve as the lowest common

[2] From *Grundbegriffe der Poetik* by Emil Staiger, Atlantis Verlag, Zürich, 1946. Reprinted by permission.

In English translation the contrast between the two stanzas is less conspicuous. Hebbel: "Come, let's pick strawberries, / The forest is, after all, not far, / Let's pluck young roses, / For they wither so fast!" Staiger: "Let's pick strawberries, / The forest isn't far, / And pluck young roses, / Roses wither so fast."

denominator of songlike lyric poems), no one will assume "the conformity between that which exists and the poet," nor feel inclined to theorize about the temporal or atemporal nature of lyric "remembrance." Nevertheless, the modified text corroborates important characteristics suggested by Staiger's description of the lyric. The solid kernel of this description may be paraphrased as follows: (1) A predominantly lyric work of literature evokes a mood without being specific or explanatory about it. (2) The speaker of the text does not emerge from this mood to the point of establishing a distance between himself and the objects he names or between himself and the persons he addresses. (3) A verbal rhythm definite enough to suggest a kind of humming, but vague enough to preclude wearisome declamation, is best suited to serve lyric purposes. One may object that even this version of Staiger's concept of the lyric style focuses on the songlike poems of Goethe and the German romanticists, and largely disregards the lyric achievements of such "learned" or difficult poets as Horace, Donne, Hölderlin, and Mallarmé. This neglect has indeed provoked some justified criticism in the last two decades. Still, I believe that Staiger's remarks on the lyric convincingly characterize one important kind of lyric poetry and thus yield insights into the generic stratification of literature.

According to Staiger, an attitude of distance (*Abstand, Gegenüber*) characterizes epic style. The act of detached presentation (*Vorstellung*) clearly separates "object" from "subject," the well-articulated epic world from its leisurely chronicler. Whereas in the lyric a great variety of flexible rhythmical patterns embody unique moods, Homer's unyielding hexameter suggests a firm standpoint from which events and characters of the past have been re-presented (*vergegenwärtigt*). In the majority of Homer's lines, the rhythmical unit corresponds to a paratactical unit of meaning which, in further contrast to the lyric flux, preserves a high degree of independence from the preceding as well as the ensuing sentence. Staiger associates Homer's version of polytheism and of the social fabric of Greece with the paratactical vision of "the epic." Zeus among the gods (as well as Agamemnon among the Greek leaders) rules as *primus inter pares* rather than an absolute monarch. Furthermore, Staiger argues that Homer's expanded similes and episodic plots reflect the same principle—the allotment of independent significance to every part of a whole (pp. 83f, 110ff, 120f, 218f).

In order to make the individual stations of the epic journey through the world seem just as important as its final destination, the epic poet avoids stirring undue curiosity about the outcome of his stories. In the first book of the *Odyssey*, the gods decide that the hero shall return home eventually. Later, Odysseus relates his most perilous adventures: himself the living proof of their happy ending. Naturally, the *Iliad* is even more "epic" in this respect; here, too, we know from the outset that Troy will fall, but the poem is not directly concerned with such a momentous event which would have to overshadow everything else. Indeed, Staiger adheres to the view that the *Iliad* stops rather than ends; in his opinion, the poet has not imposed general patterns on the loosely connected series of events, nor on the characterization of the figures who never change or mature. From his analysis of Homer, Staiger concludes that, at the early stage of civilizations, the epic functions as a kind of stocktaking; its unrestrained concern for individual detail establishes the necessary basis for man's gradually developing interest in relationships and universal significance. In contrast to the epic attitude, the Christian view of the world could be termed hypotactical because it considers man and his universe as fully dependent on the divine; consequently, it permits genuine epic only in special cases. God is palpably absent from the realm of the Devil: this alone allows Dante's "Inferno" as well as the hell scenes of Milton and Klopstock to approach Staiger's ideal of the epic; except for the subhuman characters of the medieval beast epics, only the damned do not partake in the upward motion of the Christian universe and remain eternally the same (pp. 107f, 127, 132, 135ff).

The pivotal concepts of Staiger's chapter on the epic style are firmly rooted in the German critical tradition. Staiger quotes Schiller on the autonomy of parts, Hegel on the historical background of the preoccupation with seemingly unrelated details, Vischer on the epic distance. Other aspects of Staiger's theory seem to have been suggested by Wilhelm von Humboldt, August Wilhelm Schlegel, Jean Paul Richter, and Goethe. But whereas Staiger succeeds in incorporating many observations of his German predecessors into his own suggestive account of Homer's style, he ignores the non-German criticism of Homer as well as all modern theories of narrative literature. This is unfortunate since, to mention only one example, Percy Lubbock's concepts of "scenic" and "panoramic" narration could have helped Staiger to relate Homer's style to other narrative methods in a more even-tempered fashion. As Thomas M. Greene has convincingly argued in *The Descent from Heaven* (1963), the great epic poem often invokes moral issues and the historical context in scenic rather than panoramic manner (pp. 19ff). This explains, I believe, quite a few of the Homeric traits Staiger contrasts to the style of later prose fiction: the apparent distance between narrator and events, the autonomy of loosely connected details, the impression that past events are *re-*

presented, and the neglect of character development. Yet Staiger describes the "epic style" in the exclusive terms of such scenic characteristics of the great epic poem and interprets their absence from novels and short stories as the result of lyric or dramatic (rather than simply panoramic) trends in post-Homeric narrative literature.

Staiger's exposition of what he terms "the dramatic" seems to me his least useful contribution to modern genre criticism. He redefines the words "pathos" and "problem" to indicate two poles of the dramatic style: "pathos" affects a man's will as the compelling force of that which shall be; "problem," in a sense suggested by the word's etymology, is something cast ahead to be overtaken. In Staiger's view, "pathos" and "problem," that is to say will and search, are fundamentally allied because both are directed toward the future (pp. 151, 160, 171). Yet his labored argument fails to eliminate the basic dissimilarity between the illustrations he provides for the two versions of the dramatic. Epigrams and fables with a punch line solving their "problem" suggest an attitude completely different from the mood of a "pathetic" tragedy, *Novelle*, or ode. It may be conceded that the suicide Heinrich von Kleist, Staiger's chief witness for the tragic personal consequences of a consistently "dramatic" worldview, connects motifs of will and search in many of his dramatic and narrative works (pp. 190f). It is also true that procreation, oracles, premonitions, and other pointers to the future help shape the plot structure in a large number of plays as well as in Kleist's "Michael Kohlhaas" and "Die Marquise von O," to mention only two supposedly dramatic *Novellen*. Yet such shared characteristics in the worlds evoked by otherwise very different literary works cannot be convincingly interpreted in Staiger's predominantly "expressive" system of generic classification. I regret that Staiger has by-passed the significant difference between the reliance of drama on the dialogue form and the more complex verbal medium of narrative fiction; the playwright's ostensible avoidance of authorial intervention in the imaginative product of his mind might have provided helpful clues for a theory of generic "attitudes."

In close connection with his concept of the dramatic, Staiger treats the tragic and the comic as philosophical or psychological rather than literary phenomena. The "dramatic" question: "What for?" (*Wozu?*) leads to the establishment of a "world," a unified system of values, in a man's consciousness. The construction of such a world, however, results from the precarious rashness (*Voreiligkeit*) of a finite being since, within the confines of human existence, "no god is so wise and great" that a man could orient his life toward this one god only without offending or betraying other gods. If the "world," an accepted frame of ethical reference, "breaks" amidst the unremitting attacks of the prodding question "What for?" we encounter the tragic. The reconciliation at the conclusion of many tragedies intimates that the elements of the broken world may crystallize in a new order; in contrast, the comic simply turns the original question "What for?" into an ironic "What on earth for?" (*Wozu auch?*). Like the tragic, it makes us aware of the limitations of finite human beings, but this awareness is not painful since it results in abandoning the exacting struggle against those limitations. The tragic exhibits man's desire for order—his ever incomplete design of *the* world—in the state of frustration. The comic in turn suggests that the troublesome desire itself can be happily ignored if we are willing to abide by our human boundaries (pp. 183, 186ff, 192, 198f). I concede that this rather Hegelian interpretation of the tragic and the comic may further the study of literature beyond the limits of specific genres of drama. Yet Staiger has disengaged his concepts of the tragic and the comic from the verbal structure of drama at a price: he has chosen to ignore the great generic significance of dialogue. As a result, Staiger's concept of the dramatic unifies his metadramatic interpretation of the tragic and the comic but sheds very little light on the nontragic and noncomic aspects of drama.

It is astonishing how little Staiger's numerous references to literary theories help locate his *Grundbegriffe* on the critical scene of the last decades. As far as literary theory is concerned, the German writers and estheticians of the late eighteenth and the early nineteenth centuries are his guiding stars. The breeze of twentieth-century ideas reaches Staiger's generic concepts from the groves of contemporary philosophy rather than criticism. Having attempted to illuminate the meaning of the adjectives *lyrisch*, *episch*, and *dramatisch* as they are used by "educated German-speaking people of our time," Staiger proceeds to suggesting that the three styles are literary manifestations of basic human attitudes and that, accordingly, his theory of genre can be considered as a contribution of literary criticism to "philosophical anthropology" (pp. 240, 253f). In a rather stimulating manner, Staiger likens "the lyric," "the epic," and "the dramatic" to the three phases of language distinguished in the first volume of Ernst Cassirer's *Philosophie der symbolischen Formen* (1923): the sensuous, the intuitive, and the conceptual phase. This analogy at once separates and interrelates the three stylistic types; on the literary level of organization, the emotive, semantic, and syntactical units of language (in Staiger's transcription: syllable, word, and sentence) always cooperate, and it is plausible that the relative importance of the three phases should make a literary work predominantly lyric, epic, or dramatic (pp. 208f).

Staiger's recourse to the ontological analysis of care (*Sorge*) in Martin Heidegger's *Sein und Zeit* (1927) is more laborious. It seems to me highly doubtful whether criticism can profit from Staiger's assumption that the dramatic style corresponds to Heidegger's future-bound concept of "understanding" (*Verstehen*); the lyric style to the preteritive "state of mind" (*Befindlichkeit*); and the epic style to "falling" (*Verfallen*) with its present implications (pp. 219ff). Staiger's own conceptual equivalents for the three generic attitudes summarize his stylistic observations in a more natural manner. At successive stages of his argument, the following triads [3] are employed to designate the essence of the lyric, the epic, and the dramatic style:

Das Lyrische	Das Epische	Das Dramatische
Erinnerung	Vorstellung	Spannung (titles of chapters)
Einflößen	Fesseln	Spannen (pp. 48, 118)
eingegeben	gesammelt	erzwungen (p. 78)
Fühlen	Zeigen	Beweisen (p. 210)
Erinnern	Vergegenwärtigen	Entwerfen (p. 217)
Seele	Körper(-lichkeit)	Geist (pp. 210f, 214)

As a penetrating critic, Staiger applies these metaphors with a great deal of sensitivity. In the limelight of isolation, however, they betray considerable affinity with less useful expressive typologies, most notably with Theophil Spoerri's. Strangely enough, Staiger does not even mention that Spoer-

---

[3] Some connotations of the German words will not survive translation: remembrance, presentation, tension; instill, captivate, suspend; intimated, amassed, exacted; feeling, showing, proving; remembering, representing, projecting; soul, body, spirit.

ri's *Präludium zur Poesie* (1929) expounded *das Epische, das Lyrische,* and *das Dramatische* as poetic expression in static, dynamic, and normative form, considered "manifold combinations" of the three types, and related them to three "views of reality" involving Staiger's triad—also found in the generic speculations of Novalis—body, soul, and spirit. Correspondences between Ernst Hirt's and Staiger's analyses of the epic distance and of the lyric lack of distance are less striking because of their obviously shared indebtedness to the German critical tradition. Another interesting parallel emerges, however, when Staiger suggests (as did Ernest Bovet, p. 249, in 1911) an analogy between the cardinal colors of the solar spectrum and the generic types of literature (p. 215). Remembering that Bovet and Spoerri taught and Hirt studied at Staiger's *alma mater*, one may be tempted to speak of a local tradition of predominantly "expressive" genre concepts at the University of Zurich.

Staiger's influence is, of course, not limited to one Swiss university. His theory has been widely discussed and, particularly by German scholars, welcomed as the most coherent post-Crocean revival of the philosophical ambitions of Romantic genre criticism. It is only in the last fifteen years or so that German critics of the "East" as well as the "West" seem to have become impatient with the traditional division of literature, be it into lyric, epic, and dramatic genres, be it into three corresponding attitudes. In "Literaturforschung vor neuen Aufgaben" (1956), Joachim G. Boeckh bluntly condemns the "narrow fold" of the tripartite classification as erected by "late bourgeois estheticism." Boeckh pleads for establishing a conceptual framework more hospitable to such genres as the essay, the feuilleton, the puzzle, the formal address, the newspaper report, the polemical satire, and the proverb. As Willi Flemming's article, "Das Problem der Dichtungsgattung und -art" (1959), indicates, genuinely inspired representatives of those genres may enter a somewhat extended "fold" and share its fourth corner, "meditative literature" (*Gedankendichtung*), with such crossbred or runaway goats from the other three flocks as the epigram, the parable, and the morality play. Without endorsing any specific fourfold classification, Friedrich Sengle's *Literarische Formenlehre* (1967) also advocates the claim of different kinds of "applied literature" (*Zweckformen*) to more serious attention than critics in the tradition of Goethe's three *Naturformen der Dichtung* can be expected to devote to them. Apparently unaware of the Chicago Aristotelians' distinction between didactic and mimetic literature, Boeckh, Flemming, Sengle, and some other German critics interested in the history and theory of the essay and related genres clearly focus on what Elder Olson discussed as the thematic aspect of speech as *lexis*.

Two books turn the dissatisfaction with the lyric-epic-dramatic approach into more detailed suggestions. Tentatively reviving the fourfold classification of some preromantic critics, Herbert Seidler's manual, *Die Dichtung* (1960), adds *Didaktik* to the familiar triad. In curious subjugation to several tripartite theories upon which he attempts to improve, Seidler contrasts *contemplation* to lyric introspection, epic observation, and dramatic fascination as the didactic "attitude," *showing* to singing, narrating, and representing as the didactic artist's particular mode of shaping his verbal material, and the didactic *construction of an ordered whole* to the lyric poet's expression of immediate experience, the epic writer's detached and the playwright's involved presentation of events (pp. 344ff, 369, 438ff).

More original in purpose and terminology is Wolfgang

Victor Ruttkowski's study, *Die literarischen Gattungen* (1968), even though little more than his reasonably international bibliography indicates that Ruttkowski studied in Canada and teaches in the United States. Rarely modifying Staiger's three "basic concepts," Ruttkowski postulates a fourth attitude, the "artistic," as present in all and predominant in some works of literature. He locates the lyric, epic, and dramatic "points of orientation" in the poet's inner world, exterior reality, and intrinsic plot structure, adding to this rather conventional list that predominantly artistic works are oriented toward the implied receiver of their message. Without reference to Northrop Frye's similar distinction between "internal" and "external" fiction—the hero's and the writer's relationship to their respective societies—Ruttkowski distinguishes between two kinds of I-Thou relationship: verbal communication between dramatic characters and the writer's direct appeal to spectators, listeners, or readers. The latter kind of relationship underlies the "artistic attitude" prevailing in essays, sermons, aphorisms, dedicatory epistles, cabaret songs, and other genres usually considered polemical or didactic. Ruttkowski argues convincingly that no literary work is completely devoid of marks of its author's consideration of a potential audience. To illustrate the secondary, yet important function of the "artistic attitude" in works fundamentally informed by some other attitude, Ruttkowski refers to Thomas Mann's ironic novels, Erich Kästner's satirical poems, and Bertolt Brecht's plays full of songs *ad spectatores* and other "alienation effects" (pp. 45, 76, 87, 129).

Ruttkowski postulates a trend of gradual increase in complexity and sophistication from the lyric through the epic and the dramatic up to the artistic attitude which he considers most akin to the dramatic member of the familiar generic triad (p. 103). Indeed, he likens the author of predominantly "artistic" works to a "performing artist who shifts his attention from the work to the audience" (p. 87). To be sure, dramatic works often contain such direct appeals to the audience as Aristophanes's choral parabases and the sung or spoken asides of individual characters. Yet Ruttkowski's theory fails to do justice to a simple fact of which he is naturally aware: those direct appeals can be very effective in plays precisely because they are diametrically opposed to drama's fundamental generic illusion. Far from establishing direct verbal contact between writer and reader, most plays evoke their fictive world as fully independent both of the author and of the audience. In contrast, the reader of lyric poetry and narrative fiction often "listens" to spokesmen of the implied author. I think, therefore, that Ruttkowski could have given us a more convincing account of the artistic attitude, had he stressed its affinity with the "attitudes" informing those two types of nondramatic literature.

2. *Pragmatic Concepts*

The generic concepts to be surveyed next propose to explain similarities between literary works with regard to the effect of the works on a reader's mind. The earliest twentieth-century instances of such a "pragmatic" orientation can be found throughout Th. A. Meyer's investigation of *Das Stilgesetz der Poesie* (1901). In striking contrast to Croce's universal *Esthetics*, Meyer elaborates on the *specific* qualities of literature as the "art of supersensory verbal imagination." Disputing the widely held tenet that literature addresses itself to the reader's inner vision, Meyer insists that not perceptual images but the very words and thoughts of language function as "the means of literary representation." He who says "nose" does not "show" us the rest of the face, nor do the words "red nose" indicate the exact hue and shape of a nose; in brief, the totality of visual perception lies beyond the reach of language whose "fragmentary" images can only be thought, not seen (pp. IV, 9, 39, 42).

Due to its highly abstract nature, language—this "marvelous abbreviation of reality"—guides the reader's receptive activity along conceptual rather than perceptual lines. Yet the dialogue form of drama promotes the reader's identification with the fictional characters to the point of fully awakening his "mimic impulse" (*mimischer Trieb*) which then strives to turn mental identification into a physical experience (*körperliches Miterleben*). Obviously enough, no reader achieves bodily identification with the characters. Therefore, only the theatrical performance of a drama can provide undisturbed enjoyment. On the stage, plays cease to be "beautiful torsos" which incite the mimic impulse without satisfying it; the actor's performance gives the natural impulse the dignity of art and eliminates the "incorporeal one-sidedness" of printed drama by adding body to the utterances of the Soul (pp. 107ff).

In contrast to drama's reliance on the art of the theater, lyric and narrative works check the power of the mimic impulse by means of literary devices. Although the lyric poet, at least grammatically, identifies himself with the "lyric I" (*lyrisches Subjekt*), the reader of his poem does not experience a strong mimic impulse because, unlike the reader of drama, he is not made to witness the actual emergence of emotions; the emotions appear to have been there before the speaker of the poem begins to talk. "Epos" (by which term Meyer refers to all narrative literature) precludes excessive identification in another way. Its reporting form of presentation places the reader at a distance from the fictional charac-

ters, and the narrative emphasis on the exterior circumstances
of action further supports him in assuming the attitude of a
detached spectator rather than that of an involved actor (pp.
109f, 196f, 229).

To be sure, Meyer's generic concepts are not central to the
stimulating argument of his book and give the impression of
tentative extemporizations. Furthermore, the crucial term
"mimic impulse" appears today as a fancy result of out-
dated pseudopsychological speculation. It should be noted,
however, that the demand to account for the specific, so to
speak metaliterary, effect of drama on its readers and spectators is still with us; and Francis Fergusson's influential *Idea
of a Theater* (1949) has introduced a concept, the "histrionic
sensibility," which is closely related to Meyer's "mimic impulse": both terms refer to man's immediate response to his
direct perception of action.

An interesting theory of verbal communication underlies
Wolf Dohrn's generic concepts expounded in *Die künstlerische Darstellung als Problem der Ästhetik* (1907). Whoever
hears words without seeing the speaker cannot help wondering about their source; from this observation Dohrn infers
that words, in addition to functioning as signs, always point
to a person whose utterances they are. No strict grammatical
rule but the listener's or reader's mode of perception, guided
of course by the text itself, defines the respective importance
of signification and expression in every instance of verbal
communication; we are induced either to concentrate on the
data of the communication or else to relate the data to a
speaker's consciousness. In the former case, the communication assumes the form of a "report" (*Bericht*); in the latter,
it primarily functions as an "utterance" (*Äußerung*). In the
area of utterance Dohrn distinguishes two kinds of relation-

ship between the speaker's experience and its objects. Ordinary utterances do not suggest that they have sprung from experience simultaneous with the act of talking. But the highest form of utterance, "manifestation" (*Kundgabe*), does precisely that and thus affects the listener as a complete interpenetration of the subject matter and the experiential basis of the communication (pp. 55, 59, 64f). Dohrn does not explicitly connect his three general modes of perception of words with the triad "epic," "lyric," and "dramatic perception." It seems clear, however, that he describes the three literary modes of perception with regard to his previously delineated concepts of report, utterance, and manifestation.

The "objective" novel of the later nineteenth century has determined Dohrn's concept of "epic perception." He likens the epic writer to a glass window through which we look at a landscape; the window can only give its color to the landscape, but even this contribution remains unnoticed for the time of our "esthetic enjoyment." Dohrn does not dispute that the detached critic, contemplating the work as an "artistic object" (*künstlerischer Gegenstand*), would discern the writer's thoughts, images, and feelings in it; yet he insists that the "epic perception" of an involved reader responds to an integrated "esthetic object" (*ästhetischer Gegenstand*) from which the narrator of the story does not emerge as an independent entity (pp. 11, 75). That such a view of narration fails to account for moralizing passages or direct addresses to the reader, goes without saying.

Dohrn describes dramatic perception as informed by the dialogue form of drama. Constantly associating words with the consciousness of a speaker, the reader or spectator of a play perceives human beings as they manifest themselves in and through the expressive elements of their speech. The technique of epistolary novels functions in a similar manner; in accordance with Goethe's dictum about the dramatic nature of this genre, Dohrn analyses *Die Leiden des jungen Werthers* (1774) as a primarily dramatic work in which the contents of the hero's letters are perceived by the reader as the experience of a concrete, well-defined individual (pp. 79f, 118ff, *et passim*).

Lyric perception is different. Metaphorically speaking, it corresponds to the "gaseous state" of lyric "moods, images, thoughts, and emotions"; instead of connecting the utterances to a clearly envisaged personality with a past and a future, it accepts the "lyric I" as the evolving center of a highly stylized form of communication. Dohrn likens the words of drama to genuine gestures and the words of lyric poetry to figures of a dance, suggesting that the reader of lyric poems often perceives expressive values as inherent in the words themselves regardless of their speakers (pp. 82f, 85). With this criterion in mind, Dohrn argues that quasi-dramatic monologues (*Rollengedichte*) engage our lyric rather than dramatic perception; the speaker in Mörike's "Das verlassene Mägdlein," for instance, functions merely as the "necessary psychic source of the words" without assuming the dramatic dimension of a distinct person (pp. 92ff). I think that Dohrn might have developed a more flexible concept of the *Rollengedicht* and a keener awareness of the "lyric" aspects of poetic drama, had he consistently employed his initial concept of manifestation—the "highest form of utterance" rather than a completely independent third mode of communication—in his analysis of dramatic perception.

Some eminently "pragmatic" concepts of genre focus on the reading public's expectations. In his article "Types in

Literature" (1917), Harold Elmer Mantz suggested that "the conscious conforming by the artist to a convention which will render his work more readily understood by others" functions as an important factor in bringing about literary types (p. 476). Among the Russian Formalists, Yurij Tynjanov seems to have gone furthest in a similar direction when he argued that "it is necessary to ascertain the level of nonliterary discourse to which a given work of literature is geared." And Tynjanov's concern for genre was not limited to the "speech orientation" (*rechevaja ustanovka*) of various literary kinds; in a diagnosis of the contemporary crisis of prose fiction (1924) he terms one of the symptoms the atrophy of the "sense of genre" (*oshchushchenie zhanra*). Arguing that the relative weight of parts cannot be properly assessed if the perception of the whole of a "small" or "large" form is absent, Tynjanov insists that "without the mental image of the total dimensions of a work words have no resonator, action develops wastefully, gropingly" (pp. 204, 215).

In addition to his "expressive" considerations already discussed, Paul Van Tieghem's article, "La Question des genres littéraires" (1938), also vindicates the role of the reading public and its imperative expectations in the establishment of generic conventions. One likes to listen to beautiful stories that are nobler than vulgar reality, and the great epic poem or, later, the "idealistic novel" must meet the demand; one likes to see exact portraitures of familiar surroundings with all their meanness and ugliness, and we have the realistic novel. Similarly, the wish to be enraptured by grand and noble sentiments gives rise to the genre of the solemn ode; the desire to have vices and absurdities bantered motivates comedy and satire; and tragedy satisfies readers and spectators by stirring them with its spectacle of pathetic adventures. After certain genres have ceased to flourish, closely related new ones emerge employing "the same abilities of writers" and satisfying "the same preferences of the public." According to this suggestive image of a relay race of literary kinds, the Homeric epic and the historical novel "à la Walter Scott," the courtly romance in verse and the psychological novel, the *tragédie classique* and modern prose drama, respectively, constitute "not formal but psychological genres" (I, 99).

At the Lyons Congress of Literary History (1939), Pierre Kohler also gave an interesting "pragmatic" turn to his (at first predominantly "expressive") "Contribution à une philosophie des genres." Aware of the function of the book as a "social bond" (*lien social*), Kohler points out that, "brutally speaking," genres might be regarded as contracts between producers and consumers of art. The writer-producer observes "the discipline of the genres" so that he can "deliver beauty, emotion, reflections, reasons to grow enthusiastic, and means to feel alive, in an accessible form without upsetting the reader's habits and decorum." The commercial metaphor may sound debasing, but it is hard to deny that compliance with some generic "contract" needs to protect even the most subtle or dignified message of an artist from "getting lost in a deaf solitude" (II, 142).

In "Literary Forms and Types" (1941), Norman H. Pearson reduced many expressive and pragmatic views to a quotable formula: genres "may be regarded as institutional imperatives which both coerce, and are in turn coerced by, the writer." Pearson convincingly argues that "the problem of the writer is not only what he would like to do but also what the public insists shall be done" (pp. 59ff, 70). On the evidence of "Qu'est-ce que la Littérature?" (1947) we may assume that Jean-Paul Sartre would endorse Pearson's conclusion. In that well-known essay Sartre calls reading "directed creation" (*création dirigée*) and argues that the examining magistrate in Dostoevski's *Crime and Punishment* would not "exist" without the reader's hatred, lent to Raskolnikov, against him. On this view, creative writing is an appeal to the reader's freedom to give "objective existence" to disclosures made by means of language (II, 95f).

In order to strengthen his plea for "engaged literature" at least in the realm of prose, Sartre concedes that it is impossible for genuine lyric poetry to be "engaged." In his opinion, the poet's words resemble the painter's colors and the composer's tones: they *are* rather than signify. Prose, in turn, is the "empire of signs." Like any person who speaks, the prose writer "uses" words not as objects but as designations of objects; his discourse proceeds (like speech) as a kind of action (II, 60, 63, 70f). This clear-cut separation of engaged prose from detached poetry must be seen as the result of polemical simplification. In a somewhat reluctant footnote (II, 87f) Sartre himself admits that words are never *exclusively* employed as either things or signs. Yet he fails to realize that his prosodic distinction between verse and prose cannot even serve to determine whether the words of a given work *primarily* "are" or "signify."

It is fortunate that certain considerations in "Qu'est-ce que la Littérature?" provide clues to Sartre's implicit idea of a more subtle classification of literature as well. This classification is outlined in a nutshell when Sartre refers to writers in general as *l'essayiste, le romancier, le poète* (II, 164) and is further elaborated upon in his comments on works by the eminently "engaged" writers Vercors and Richard Wright. As to *Le Silence de la mer* (1941), Sartre argues that Vercors, writing for a defeated and occupied France, had to treat the German soldiers as human beings, good or bad or rather good *and* bad at the same time, in order to prove the necessity of resistance even though some Germans might appear "men like you and I." Similarly, Richard Wright used the fact that his public was "split" (*déchiré*) as "the pretext for a work of art." Had he written only for the whites, his *Black Boy* (1945) would have approached didactic satire; had he written only for the blacks, it would have come close to "prophetic lamentations"— Sartre recalls that Jeremiah spoke only to the Jews. It was on account of a radical change in the situation of its readers that Vercors's novel lost its "efficacy" at the end of 1942; by that time, the active resistance as well as the retaliatory measures had eliminated the difference between accomplices and victims of Nazism among the German soldiers, and it became natural to think of all Germans in the black-and-white images of propaganda broadcast from London or whispered in the streets of Paris (II, 120ff, 125ff). Thus Sartre's thesis about all works containing "the image of the reader for whom they were meant" (II, 119) seems to call for a bipartition in the realm of "prose." From genres exhibiting the writer's overtly biased engagement (essay, pamphlet, satire, prophecy), a more detached and discreet form of *littérature engagée* (with the novel as its most important modern representative) can be distinguished.

In his early criticism, of course, Sartre explicitly refused to accept a "sum of signs and intentions" as a novel. In 1938 he likened novels to things—comparable to paintings or works of architecture—made of "free minds" (*consciences libres*) and "time" (*durée*). In agreement with Ramon Fernandez's distinction between the "account" (*récit*) of past events and the genuine novel, Sartre remarked that "the novel, like life, unfolds in the present" and that the novelist should neither explain the past of his characters nor allow their future to appear as determined in advance. Narrated things and events must "retain the flavor of the present" and remain what they once were—"inexplicable tumults of color, sound, and passion." Yet Sartre also argued that if a book presents a "series of happenings without rhyme and reason," it is apt to make us wonder about "the secret intentions of the author"; only if the "necessities of the plot" motivate the sequence of events will the reader "lose his footing" and identify himself with a character's perspective instead of contemplating the world of fiction from without (I, 7, 16f, 56, 141f). One may conclude that the presence of fictional figures whose point of view the reader cannot help but share makes the difference between the essayist's and the romancier's "prose," and the same distinction suggests itself between a totally "engaged" drama and one in which the undistorted internal perspective of a plot prevails. If the author of the latter type of drama or a genuine novelist incorporates an engaged message in the "objective" (and not merely "signifying") structure of his work, he combines aspects of Sartre's allegedly disparate genres—disengaged poetry and activist prose.

In the Introduction to her *Logik der Dichtung* (1957), Käte Hamburger proposes to place literary works in the system of verbal communication just as a theory of esthetics places them in the system of the arts. With frequent references to the larger context of discourse, Miss Hamburger's "logic of literature" charts the area of literary art in the form of an original theory of genre. This theory primarily relies on the assumption that readers respond in two disparate ways to two disparate kinds of literary works; while narrative and dramatic literature elicit an "experience of nonreality," lyric poems impress us as "statements concerning reality" (*Wirklichkeitsaussagen*). In support of her argument, Miss Hamburger suggests that Aristotle excluded lyric poems from the *Poetics* because they did not fit in with his mimetic theory of *poesis* as the "making" of actions and characters. By the same token, Miss Hamburger contrasts lyric poetry as the "existential" genre presenting "a subject's statements about objects" to the "mimetic" genres —narrative and dramatic literature—in which fictive subjects are being "engendered" (pp. 2f, 7ff, 146, 181).

Since her concept of *mimesis* is more difficult to uphold with regard to narrative fiction than with regard to drama, Miss Hamburger rightly concentrates on the elucidation of what she calls "epic fiction." To begin with, she contrasts historical or ordinary to mimetic narration. In brief, the "historical I" of textbooks, reports, autobiographies, and the like makes correct or incorrect statements about real events or about events believed to be real. The mimetic narrator, however, asserts nothing and thus neither tells the truth nor lies. Instead of predicating about facts, he creates "subjects" —beings who will say "I" themselves—and disappears behind them. Just as human figures in a painting are but painted figures, the characters in a narrative work are narrated characters, for the mimetic narrator narrates *them* and not (as a historical chronicler would) *about* them. As a result, he enters the world of fiction as a more or less neutral "function of narration" (*Erzählfunktion*): his narration is nothing but the narrated action, and the narrated action is nothing but his narration (pp. 21ff, 75f, 100).

Miss Hamburger describes mimetic narration by perceptibly elaborating on three salient features of this kind of discourse: the occasional designation of space and time from the point of view of the fictive characters, the employment of the "epic preterit" without imparting to the reader a sense of the past, and the frequent evocation of "subjective events" occuring in the mind of a character (pp. 56, 74, *et passim*). In Miss Hamburger's thoroughgoing investigation, mostly German texts of considerable length illustrate each of those important points. For our purposes, the following sentence of my own making will suffice:

> Assuming his usual attitude of greater experience, Jack glanced at Mary and started to imagine how quickly his greenhorn brother would fall in love with this blonde at the party tonight.

All three basic characteristics of Miss Hamburger's "mimetic narration" can be observed in the above sample. First, Jack's fictional stance in space and time represents the point of reference for the pronoun 'this' and the adverb 'tonight.' Next, despite the preterite tense of the finite verbs, the reader is not invited to picture Jack's actions ('glanced') and thoughts ('started to imagine') as past events in relation to the writer's or his own "present." Rather, Jack's own, of course fictive, awareness of being involved in a present event is evoked in the responsive reader's mind. Finally, the phrase 'started to imagine' characterizes the sentence as "mimetic" since such a reference to "subjective events" could not occur in a strictly "historical" context—a history of Great Britain or a testimony in a murder case, for example—without impairing the narrator's general credibility. All of this granted, we should not fail to notice that the point of view prevailing in the sentence is not altogether Jack's. Whereas the words 'this' and 'tonight' evoke his "subjective stance" as the point of orientation, the designations 'Jack' (instead of 'I') and 'his . . . brother' (instead of 'my brother,' the brother's name, or the pronoun 'he') reveal a narrative perspective external to Jack's subjectivity. Furthermore, the use of 'would' instead of 'will' characterizes the last words as *oratio obliqua* and thus points to a "speaker" who quotes what Jack thinks. Surely, Jack's fictive perception of the color of Mary's hair and the narrator's "opinion" of that color concur to the extent of making it doubtful whether we should distinguish two minds as different psychological sources of the meaning of the word 'blonde.' Yet the word 'greenhorn' functions in the ironic mode of substitutionary narration [4] and therefore carries the full weight of a double charge; in its context, that simple word at once manifests Jack's opinion of his brother and the ironic distance from which the narrator views this opinion. In an earlier account (1951) of her concept of mimetic narration, Miss Hamburger showed considerable awareness of the fact that substitutionary narration (according to German terminology: *erlebte Rede*) grammatically integrates a fictive character's vision with the writer's (pp. 24f). It is unfortunate that her *Logik der Dichtung* does not do similar justice to the *dual* rather than purely figural perspective informing most passages of "mimetic narration." Her concept of the "function of narration" helps her avoid the customary pitfall of abstracting the storyteller from the story. At the same time, Miss Hamburger seems to ignore that the *function* of nar-

[4] Cf. Appendix: "Free Indirect Discourse and Related Techniques."

ration as a function of *narration* presupposes the vision of a narrator as one constituent of the dual perspective informing narrative works.

In contrast to this dual perspective, the spatial, temporal, and grammatical orientation of the fictive characters thoroughly prevails in the direct speech of dramatic dialogue. In a somewhat crudely dramatized version of the story of Mary, Jack, and his brother, our friend would exclaim: "I know that my brother will fall in love with this blonde at the party tonight!" In spite of the "dramatic" immediacy of the pronouns and tenses of such an utterance, Miss Hamburger rightly insists that the text of plays (or even the massive "here and now" of a performance) does not affect us in an unduly literal way; after all, no spectator thinks of the day after the performance when he hears an actor say "I will show her the letter tomorrow." Miss Hamburger's resolutely atemporal concept of "fictionalization" thus encompasses both the mimetic narrator's "epic preterit" and the apparent "present" of dialogue in narrative works and plays. Nevertheless, her idea of drama seems to me rashly deduced from her concept of narrative literature. As she considers plays as works of mimetic fiction in which "the function of narration has become equal to nil" (pp. 119f, 130), Miss Hamburger overlooks the structural significance of the playwright's "side texts" ranging from the laconic but necessary indication of the respective speakers through elaborate stage directions to explanatory prefaces. I believe that a consistent logic of literature should either hold the view that dialogue *plus* staging constitute the finished products of dramatic art or else regard the entire written text (that is, the fictive dialogue *plus* the authorial statements of the "side text") as an integrated, albeit not homogeneous, verbal structure. Instead, Miss Hamburger's concept of dramatic fiction wavers between the former and the latter view. She would call stage and actor "part of the mimetic function of the playwright" and still declare a little later that they do not belong to the writer's work and transcend his competence (p. 131). But neither in a book nor on stage do plays warrant both parts of Miss Hamburger's twofold tenet according to which "word becomes character and character becomes word" in dramatic literature. Clearly, the text of all plays contains words that are not spoken by any of the *dramatis personae*, and every performance of a play adds nonverbal aspects to characterization. Only the isolated "main text" of plays, their dialogue, justifies Miss Hamburger's opinion that language in drama "becomes" the characters themselves like the sculptor's marble becomes the statue (pp. 119f).

Miss Hamburger's concept of lyric poetry is based on the observation that the speaker in lyric poems appears to make genuine statements. His words are not mere "material" of which fictive characters can be made, but emerge from the existential "field of force" (*Kraftfeld*) of subjective experience (pp. 169, 182). Miss Hamburger argues that poetic diction and metric form do not always help identify the speaker of lyric poems as a "lyric I" rather than the "historical I" of ordinary statements, the "theoretical I" of philosophy and the sciences, or a "practical I" envisaging some actual purpose. In her opinion, the function of words in lyric poetry comes so close to their function in nonliterary discourse that contextual criteria alone can sometimes determine whether or not a given text is a poem. The same hymn by Novalis, for instance, invokes the image of a "lyric I" if we read it in a volume of poetry but functions as the utterance of a "practical I," a praying person, when sung at church by members of a religious community (pp. 164f, 167).

To be sure, Miss Hamburger's concept of lyric discourse as a kind of predication outside the context of reality elucidates important aspects of poetry. In obvious contrast to "historical," "theoretical," and "practical" statements, lyric poems treat of objects as they are reflected in subjective experience. Since the experienced objects of poetry do not assume independent significance, the intrinsic experiential order of the statements prevails, and language functions as a "means of expression" rather than as a "means of communication" (pp. 166f, 177). But this is true, I believe, of lyric texts regardless of the use to which they are being put in one or another context. Novalis's hymns can be employed as part of a religious service, psychotherapy, or advanced foreign language instruction without losing their literary quality —which may or may not be noticed in a given instance—as lyric poems.

Generic classifications often reveal their shortcomings through the unsatisfactory tools they provide for dealing with "exceptions." Indeed, Miss Hamburger's treatment of what she cannot help but term "special forms" (*Sonderformen*) betrays the inflexibility inherent in much of her "logic of literature." To remain faithful to her initial bipartition of literary structure, Miss Hamburger must insist that stories narrated in the first person (*Icherzählungen*) make language function in the existential mode despite the "surface" similarity between them and genuinely mimetic works of fiction (p. 208). She is certainly justified in arguing that there is no "logical" criterion by which one could distinguish a "feigned historical I" (for example, Thomas Mann's *Felix Krull*) from the truly "historical I" of an autobiography, or the feigned "lyric I" of a quasi-dramatic monologue (*Rollengedicht*) from the speaker in lyric poems (pp. 219, 222). It seems to me, however, that the very lack of such a logical criterion should serve as a warning against too much confidence in generic concepts relying on a "logic of literaure." Indeed, Miss Hamburger's concern for logical or "inner" structure (as opposed to esthetic or "surface" form) induces her to consider all ballads and many novels which combine first-person and scenic narration as instances of logical discrepancy between the expressive and mimetic functions of language (pp. 87ff, 216f). Yet much of the attraction of those and other works of literature results precisely from the interplay between authorial presentation and impersonating representation or, in Miss Hamburger's terminology, between the "existential" and "mimetic" principles of poetic discourse. It is unfortunate, therefore, that Miss Hamburger's thought-provoking explorations ignore the mimetic aspect of the "lyric I"—the speaker and his situation are *created* by the poet's quasi-existential discourse —as well as the authorial, "existential" theme or vision permeating every work of "mimetic fiction." [5]

[5] My discussion of Käte Hamburger's theory of genres is based on the influential first edition of her *Logik der Dichtung*. The second and revised edition of the book (1968) eliminates several inconsistencies of detail yet retains most features of the basic argument with which I have been concerned in the preceding pages.

Chapter Three

The Work and Its World

1. Structural Concepts

The term "structure" has been applied by modern critics in too many connections to be discussed here. For the purposes of this survey it seems best to consider an approach to genre structural if it focuses on similarities between the ways in which the language of different literary works evokes the esthetic appearance of a world. In this sense the most fundamental distinctions applicable to literary structure concern the minds which "mean" the meaning of a given instance of verbal communication.

(1) He refused to lend her his pencil.

(2) "Lend me your pencil." "I won't."

(3) She asked him, "Will you lend me your pencil?" and he told her that he would not.

These simple sentences illustrate three basic modes of discourse. The entire meaning of *monologues* (1) points to a single "meaner." If, however, more than one "meaner" emerges from a sequence of words, the semantic tension of *dialogue* (2) informs the given text, provided no "meaner" reduces the others to secondary semantic importance by rendering their words in a direct or indirect form of *quotation* (3). Identifying both the single "meaner" of a monologue and the primary "meaner" of more complex texts with the actual speaker or writer of the words, Socrates in Plato's *Republic* distinguished three styles of literary discourse: authorial, figural, and mixed speech (Book Three, 392c and d). In his classification of literature according to the "manner of mimesis," Aristotle was perhaps the first but surely not the last critic to adopt the Socratic distinctions (*Poetics*, Chapter Three, 1448a). Indeed, post-Renaissance men of letters tend to model their generic classifications at large after those famous Greek tripartitions of "style"—the manner rather than the matter of discourse. Following the lead of A. S. Minturno's *De Poeta* (1559), Cervantes and Cascales in Spain, Milton and Dryden in England, La Motte and Batteux in France meant genres rather than styles or modes of discourse when they referred to lyric, epic, and dramatic (or scenic) literature. Around 1800, the Schlegel brothers, Schelling, Goethe, Jean Paul Richter, Hegel, and other German writers and philosophers finally established something like a doctrine of holy trinity in modern genre criticism. (Cf. Irene Behrens, *Die Lehre von der Einteilung der Dichtkunst*, 1940, *passim*.)

Fusing (if not confusing) "expressive," "pragmatic," "mimetic," and "structural" considerations, the familiar tripartition of literature into poetry, fiction, and drama can hardly be considered Platonic or Aristotelian. Nevertheless, by the turn of our century it appeared to many men of letters that the classification of literary works as lyric, epic, or dramatic had been agreed upon in all times. The esthete Stephen Dedalus in James Joyce's *Portrait of the Artist as a Young Man* (1916) even tried to extend the validity of that triad to the entire realm of art. As he explains to his friend Lynch walking beside him in the streets of Dublin, "the image, it is clear, must be set between the mind or senses of the artist himself and the mind or senses of others. If you bear this in memory you will see that art necessarily divides itself into three forms progressing from one to the next. These forms are: the lyrical form, the form wherein the artist presents his image in immediate relation to himself; the epical form, the form wherein he presents his image in mediate relation to himself and to others; the dramatic form, the form wherein he presents his image in immediate relation to others" (Chapter Five, pp. 250ff).

Observing that the three forms are least confused in literature, Stephen elaborates on generic peculiarities of this "highest and most spiritual art." In the lyric form, the personality of the writer is "a cry or a cadence or a mood"; in the epic, it is "flowing round and round the persons and the action like a vital sea"; and in the dramatic, "the vitality that has flowed and eddied around each person fills every person with such vital force that he or she assumes a proper and intangible esthetic life." Beyond doubt, the structural concepts of monologue, mixed speech, and dialogue loom large in young Stephen's theory of genre. Yet his interpretation of "the form wherein the artist presents his image in immediate relation to himself" as unmediated lyric self-expression ("the simplest verbal vesture of an instant of emotion") was by no means implied by Plato's original concept of *diegesis;* rather than Sappho's or Anacreon's "lyrics," the partly hymnal, partly narrative genre of dithyrambs served as Socrates' example of this kind of poetry.

The introduction of "expressive" aspects into the structural concept of monologue was, of course, the rule and not the exception since Sir William Jones, Johann Gottfried Herder, and other eighteenth-century writers had celebrated the lyric as the subjective source and innermost center of all poetry.

A notable exception to the "rule" can be seen in Julius Petersen's resolutely structural attempt to locate "each of the three fundamental genres" in an integrated conceptual scheme. In *Die Wissenschaft von der Dichtung* (1939), Petersen proposes to carry out Goethe's project of placing *Epos*, *Lyrik*, and *Drama* at distant points on the circumference of a circle and of arranging individual works and "poetic kinds" around the same circle according to their affinities with those three "natural forms of poetry." (Cf. *Noten und Abhandlungen zum West-Östlichen Divan*, 1819.) Obviously enough, Goethe's intention is travestied rather than realized by Petersen's elaborate wheel which, with *Epos*, *Lyrik*, and *Drama* as its spokes, contains thirty-seven "genres" around the nave representing "primordial poetry" (*Urdichtung*). Yet Petersen outlines and correlates the three traditional types of literature in a more articulated manner than does Goethe's brief discourse on the "lucidly narrating, enthusiastically excited, and personally acting" *Naturformen der Dichtung*.

Petersen describes *Epos* (by which, like Goethe, he means the prototype of all narrative literature) as the "monological report of an action," *Lyrik* as the "monological representation of a condition," and *Drama* as the "dialogical representation of an action." In their most typical forms, the epic, dramatic, and lyric genre are thus primarily characterized as report (*Bericht*), dialogue, and condition (*Zustand*). This scheme permits Petersen to assign rather plausible intermediate positions to some of his numerous subclasses within the generic wheel. An individual epistle, for instance, is a "monological report of a condition" and will appear between the spokes signifying *Lyrik* and *Epos*. The epistolary novel with several correspondents is in turn a "dialogical report of an action" and finds its place between *Epos* and *Drama* (pp. 121ff).

Implicitly acknowledging the difference between the Greek and the modern principles of generic tripartition, Albert Guérard's *Preface to World Literature* (1940) distinguishes lyric, epic, and dramatic form from lyric, epic, and dramatic spirit. With due apologies for the "fearful symmetry" of his rather tentative ninefold classification, Guérard suggests that "the lyric, the epic, the dramatic spirits, severally, can be clothed in lyric, epic, and dramatic form." The following works serve as some of his illustrations for the respective genres (pp. 197ff):

Lyrical lyric: Goethe's "Wanderers Nachtlied"
Epic (narrative) lyric: "Ballad of Sir Patrick Spence"
Dramatic lyric: Robert Browning's dramatic monologues

Lyrical epic: Byron's *Don Juan*
Epic narrative: *Iliad*
Dramatic epic: *A Tale of Two Cities*

Lyrical drama: The Tempest
Epic drama: Shelley's *Prometheus Unbound*
Dramatic drama: The "effective plays" of Scribe and
              Dumas fils—but also most plays of
              Molière and Shakespeare

Content with observing that such a classification is not in "absolute contradiction with the facts," Guérard points out that history is seldom in agreement with logic; he recommends, therefore, that we recognize not only the existence but also the looseness of literary genres. Guérard's survey of a large number of them indeed avoids the dogmatism of many critics who fail to distinguish "form" from "spirit"—the mode of literary evocation from its result, an imaginative world—and prefer what they consider pure genres (Guérard's "lyrical lyric," for example) to equally respectable kinds of literature. But his unrevoked, albeit skeptical, adherence to a threefold system of classification prevents Guérard from unifying his insights concerning proverbs, maxims, precepts, popular saws (p. 203), descriptive and philosophical poems (p. 228), personal essays, autobiographical narratives, impressionistic criticism (pp. 261ff) and oratory (pp. 302f) into the concept of a fourth type of generic form or spirit.

No skepticism attenuates Wolfgang Kayser's respect for those holy numbers of genre criticism, three and nine. In his helpful manual, *Das sprachliche Kunstwerk* (1948), Kayser distinguishes three technical "forms of presentation" (pp. 189ff), three "basic attitudes" inherent in language (pp. 330ff), and three times three "genres," each emerging from the "mysterious elective affinity" between an attitude and an "inner form" (p. 346). Contrary to Goethe and Petersen, the obvious sources of his concept of the "forms of presentation" (*Darbietungsformen*), Kayser expects this kind of classification to pigeonhole all works of literature into three unequivocal categories: narration yields epic, the action of disguised persons dramatic, the monological expression of experienced conditions lyric works. Perhaps disenchantment with such a rigid and hardly useful classification has directed Kayser's greater ambitions toward the "basic attitudes" (*Grundhaltungen*) in terms of which recent German critics like to give "expressive" interpretations to Goethe's three *Naturformen der Dichtung*. (Cf. Karl Viëtor, "Probleme der literarischen Gattungsgeschichte," p. 426.)

But Kayser's approach to the "basic attitudes" is by no means "expressive." He relates them to "three functions of language": manifestation corresponds to the lyric, communication or representation to the epic, challenge or elicitation to the dramatic attitude. These "functions" seem to me almost identical with the structural categories—expression, narration, action—underlying Kayser's classification of the "forms of presentation." Furthermore, Kayser warns against attempts to interpret lyric manifestation in connection with the poet's private life: since the author's subjectivity as such does not belong to the literary work at all, every poem must itself create the situation from which its "manifestation" issues. In view of such a resolutely impersonal concept of poetry, it is difficult to tell *whose* "basic attitudes" Kayser tries to separate from what he slights as mere "forms of presentation." In any event, his attempt to distinguish three genres within each of the three larger categories clearly transgresses the vague line of conceptual demarcation between attitude and technique. As part of his discussion of the attitudes, Kayser subdivides narrative and dramatic literature according to the predominance in individual works of the characters, the setting, or the action. Yet the resulting categories are much more intimately related to the presumably distinct techniques of *Epik* and *Dramatik* than to the epic and dramatic attitudes inherent in language. Indeed, most of Kayser's genre theory implies that the "attitudes" interpenetrate insofar as the "forms of presentation" will combine or integrate different principles of structure (pp. 332, 335f, 352ff, 368ff).

Whether forms or attitudes underlie literary genres, their necessary interplay is postulated in T. S. Eliot's lecture on *The Three Voices of Poetry* (1954). Without explicit reference to John Stuart Mill, Eliot revives Mill's concept of lyric poetry as "soliloquy overheard." In the lyric voice, Eliot argues, the poet talks to himself; part of our enjoyment of great literature results precisely from our "overhearing" words not addressed to us. Of course, the theoretician of the "objective correlative" also knows that "if the poem were exclusively for the author, it would be a poem in a private and unknown language" and, consequently, no poem at all (pp. 33f). Accordingly, Eliot is convinced that at least one of the two other voices can be heard in every lyric poem. In turn, the lyric voice must not be completely silent in works written for the second or the third voice, for "if the author never spoke to himself, the result would not be poetry, though it might be magnificent rhetoric" (p. 33). Conventionally enough, the second voice is described in terms of narration and the third voice as the vehicle of drama—the former tells a tale, the latter exhibits an action, to an audience. Yet Eliot's concept of "voice" prompts a suggestive query: does Macbeth's famous speech beginning "to-morrow, and to-morrow, and to-morrow" especially move us because "Shakespeare and Macbeth are uttering the words in unison?" (pp. 34f). And the same vocal metaphor is well suited to convey Eliot's preference for generically complex literature: "All that matters is, that in the end the voices should be heard in harmony; and I doubt whether in any real poem only one voice is audible" (p. 37).

The generic "harmony," if not indeed *polyphony*, prevailing in most literary works has been variously approached during the last few decades. Unencumbered by the preconception of a generic trinity, "structural" critics discussing a single genre often illuminate the manner in which central characteristics of different genres become integrated in the esthetic whole of individual works. Adequate treatments of the novel are especially prone to involve crucial issues of generic theory at large. Employing both narration and dialogue, the novel has inherited the "mixed" status of the great epic poem and can even surpass the original epic complexity through such devices as inserted poems, letters, diaries, or the presentation of the stream of a consciousness. Some consideration of what seem to be lyric or dramatic elements in prose fiction, lyric or epic departures in drama, and dramatic aspects of lyric poetry will help us place tripartite as well as fourfold classifications of literature in perspective.

The nineteenth-century German playwright, novelist, and critic Otto Ludwig commented on the dramatic potential of narrative fiction more systematically than Samuel Richardson, Henry Fielding, or Sir Walter Scott before him. In his posthumously published (1891) sketch entitled "Formen der Erzählung," Ludwig distinguished "narration proper" (*eigentliche Erzählung*), "scenic narration" (*szenische Erzählung*), and a combined form. By creating the impression that the storyteller experienced the narrated events or at least obtained a reliable report from someone who had witnessed them, "narrative proper" resembles ordinary accounts of actual occurrences. Its principle is the "law of memory": deviations from strict chronology must naturally follow the "association of ideas" underlying the thematic unity of the narrative. In contrast, the scenic narrator need not pretend that he can account for the source of his "information"; the sequence of vivid scenes constituting his story is, almost like a drama on the stage, capable of "telling itself." Ludwig considers "scenic narration" as a highly commendable "generic mixture" (*Mischgattung*); addressing the inner eye through the medium of the ear, it avoids both the abstract nature of "narration proper" and the cumbersome apparatus involved by the dependence of drama on the performing arts (VI, 202ff).

Ludwig celebrates the scenic narrator as the fortunate

showman who can build a theater and paint decorations to his own taste, creating actors who play but themselves. Yet Ludwig holds the third, combined form of narration in even greater favor because it can adapt itself most flexibly to the changing needs of the subsequent parts of a story. Permitting the unmediated presentation of scenes as well as the detached narrator's summaries and commentaries, the combined form adds the "charm of enigmatic suspense" (*Reiz des Problematischen*) to the appeal of clear intellectual and moral orientation. It can be "objective" as well as "subjective," both in content and in form (VI, 206).

Relying on his acquaintance with novels written, and critical insights gained, after the death of Otto Ludwig (1865), Percy Lubbock was able to make a more decisive contribution to the ensuing and still ardent interchange of views concerning *The Craft of Fiction* (1921). Lubbock argues that written literature cannot convincingly "tell" stories in the manner of oral traditions: there is an "inherent weakness" in the novelist's fictitious picture of life "if the mind that knows the story and the eye that sees it remain unaccountable" (pp. 116f). On the other hand, Lubbock knows that only the omniscient narrator's panoramic survey can cover the expanse of life which "big chronicles like Thackeray's" attempt to encompass; the narrator represents "the great principle of economy" in all stories that cannot fully express themselves in action and, therefore, call for a "picture-maker" to organize the events of their plot into "small and single impressions" (pp. 185ff, 270). Precisely because drama holds the place of honor in Lubbock's view of narrative literature, he must demand that it should not be used without a good reason: "A scene that is not really wanted and that *does* nothing in particular—a scene that for lack of preparation fails to make its effect—is a weakness in a story" (pp. 72f). Such insights mitigate Lubbock's bias against the "unaccountable" narrator, and the principle that the novelist should give to his work "the highest relief by which it is capable of profiting" may be accepted by advocates of all kinds of storytelling (p. 173).

Lubbock formulates his "structural" distinction between picture and drama as two techniques of the novel in rather "pragmatic" terms: "In one case the reader faces towards the storyteller and listens to him, in the other he turns towards the story and watches it" (p. 111). While the "talkative, confidential manner of Thackeray" illustrates Lubbock's concept of picture, he argues that the "discreet anonymous manner" in which Maupassant told many of his stories makes for "drama" because "the machinery of his telling" passes unnoticed and thus "the story appears to tell itself" (pp. 112f). Lubbock contrasts Thackeray's panoramic surveys to Maupassant's evocation of quasi-dramatic scenes without dogmatically separating the two techniques. Indeed, large sections of *The Craft of Fiction* explore characteristic combinations of picture and drama as different phases in the process of "dramatizing the picture."

The first step toward "dramatization" is to dramatize the narrator; a comparison between the omniscient storyteller of *Vanity Fair* and Thackeray's Henry Esmond telling his own story indicates how the "picture-maker" himself can become part of the picture. The epistolary novel, however, possesses greater "dramatic energy" than the autobiographical form of panoramic chronicle. Keeping Clarissa "continually bent over her pen," Samuel Richardson keeps her long ordeal in the foreground of scenes in which her emotion is "caught in passing"; she reports in such "brief and punctual intervals" that she "reveals her heart in its very pulsation" (pp. 152ff). But the most effective method of "dramatizing the picture" is employed when the writer treats a character's mind "as a play, as an action proceeding." Lubbock can convincingly argue that throughout large sections of Flaubert's *Madame Bovary* and Henry James's *The Ambassadors* the reader is not so much "told" about events as he "watches" their reflections in the "inner scene" of a consciousness (pp. 169, 256ff). Lubbock apparently prefers this subtle technique to both the "flat and thin" panoramic survey and to "drama unmixed" in which "the reader is squarely in front of the scene," unable to perceive anything directly except "the look and speech" of the characters (pp. 142, 270).

It seems to me that four distinct—yet combinable—modes of narration emerge from Lubbock's discussion of narrative structure. First the omniscient narrator's *panoramic survey* of events—a mode to be avoided whenever "there is no positive reason" for using it (p. 186). Next the mode of the *dramatized narrator* who, being actively involved in the events of the plot, will tell the story from a point of view inherent in the world of the novel. Then the *dramatic or scenic* mode in which "the story is enacted by its look and behaviour at particular moments" (p. 253). And, finally, there is the mode of the *dramatized mind* of a figure. Unaware of the first important French and German articles on substitutionary narration, Lubbock brilliantly circumscribes its ironic as well as empathic potential when he characterizes this complex narrative technique as follows: "the seeing eye is with somebody in the book," but in fact "there are now two brains behind the eye; and one of them is the author's, who adopts and shares the *position* of his creature, and at the same time supplements his wit" (p. 258).[1]

Among other novels, *Vanity Fair, Henry Esmond, Anna*

---

[1] Cf. Appendix: "Free Indirect Discourse and Related Techniques."

Karenina, and *Madame Bovary* serve as Lubbock's examples for the prevalence of the respective modes in the fabric of a narrative work. With those books in mind no one would deny that the three senses in which Lubbock speaks of drama in

1. Panoramic Survey

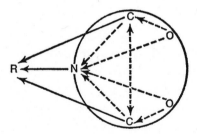

2. Dramatized Narrator

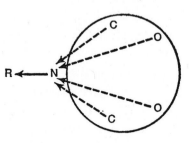

3. Scenic Narration

4. Dramatized Mind

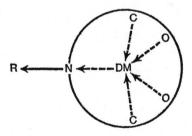

Explanations:

Circle = the world of the novel
R = reader
N = narrator
O = object (e.g., a table)
C = character
DM = dramatized mind
Dotted arrow ($\longleftarrow$----) = nonverbal information (awareness) to be transmitted to the reader through speech (the narrator's report or directly quoted dialogue) indicated by straight arrow ($\longleftarrow$)

fiction are rather divergent. Yet his three nonpanoramic modes of narration have one important thing in common; they embed the point of view from which individual parts of a story are being presented in those parts and thus in the story as a whole. In contrast, the panoramic mode relies on a narrative stance outside of what is strictly speaking the world of a given work of fiction. In the accompanying graphs I have tried to indicate important similarities and differences between the four modes.

Discussing "La Méthode de Balzac" (1926), Ramon Fernandez contrasted two poles of narrative literature in a vein strikingly similar to Percy Lubbock's distinction between the panoramic survey and the dramatic or dramatized modes of storytelling. Allowing for combinations and intermediate forms, Fernandez describes the extreme types as the "account" (*récit*), or the presentation of past events by a narrator in accordance with the principles of logic and rhetoric, and the "novel" (*roman*), or the representation of events as they emerge and develop in time. His wholesale preference for the "intuitive," "synthetic," "spontaneous," and "vital" *roman* over the "rational," "analytical," "logical," and "moralizing" *récit* betrays a somewhat literal-minded application of Henri Bergson's terminology to problems of literary criticism. Fernandez' individual observations, however, are largely free from dogmatism. Having insisted, for instance, that in a genuine novel the action seems to govern the narrator's intelligence whereas the events reported in an "account" merely illustrate rational and moral "analyses," he willingly assigns special status to quasi-autobiographical works. Some of Joseph Conrad's novels, Fernandez argues, may seem to be composed of a number of narrative accounts, yet each such "account" constitutes a "novel" because Conrad's characterized storytellers make us envision life in and through "purely esthetic syntheses." In keeping with another Bergsonian concept, Fernandez assumes the existence of *un présent non point verbal mais psychologique;* this "psychological present" (which has nothing to do with the grammatical tense of a text) may be evoked by the genuine novel's vivid representation of "imaginary scenes" or of "a character's interior life." Thus Fernandez implicitly contrasts the panoramic *récit* to three narrative techniques which resemble Lubbock's dramatized narrator, scenic narration, and dramatized mind. All three make us envision the characters' time as experienced *durée psychique* rather than conceptualized *temps* (pp. 59ff).

In a footnote to the extended and revised edition (1960) of his profound book *Das literarische Kunstwerk* (1931), Roman Ingarden indicates that distinctions between "genuine lyric, epic, and drama" could be based on the difference between particular generic modes of dealing with time (p. 257). Unfortunately, Ingarden's actual suggestions are limited to differences between narrative and dramatic literature. In narrative works, the "point zero" (*Nullpunkt*) of temporal orientation can either emerge as a constant point of retrospect or follow the progress of the story. In neither case does the reader perceive "holes" in the fabric of time because the very concept of time precludes the idea of rupture. Nevertheless, there is a fundamental difference between the retrospective orientation of "report" (*Bericht*) and the abreast temporal perspective of "another narrative technique"; while the former implies the existence of a chain of individual time phases only in a vague and indirect manner, the latter places "point zero" in the successive phases and makes the reader witness past events as though he were living "then" or, to be more exact, in the successive "now's of that time" (*in den "damaligen Jetzt"*).

Ingarden concludes that narrative works consistently adhering to the "present mode" of representation employ a method characteristic of drama (pp. 252, 256).

It might appear that Ingarden has merely reformulated Otto Ludwig's distinction between "proper" and "scenic" narration in phenomenological terms. But this new dimension of the argument is important: Ingarden points out that fictional characters fail to pass through a pre-eminent *in actu esse* phase between past and future; consequently, literary figures can easily "withdraw" from what *seems* to be their present but in fact, being "purely intentional" in Edmund Husserl's sense, corresponds to the "now-phase" in the life of real people only by analogy. Ingarden observes that narrative works can take particular advantage of the flexible structure of fictional time either by emphasizing the contemporaneousness of different events, or by viewing the same event from several different points of temporal orientation (pp. 250, 253).

Very much along the lines of Ludwig's and Ingarden's explorations, Franz Stanzel's study of narrative structure distinguishes three *Typische Erzählsituationen im Roman* (1955). Relying on his close analyses of the prevailing point of view in Fielding's *Tom Jones*, Melville's *Moby Dick*, and Henry James's *The Ambassadors*, Stanzel suggests that these works represent divergent types to be designated as *auktorialer Roman*, *Ich-Roman*, and *personaler Roman*. By addressing the reader directly or adding personal comments as such to the action, the narrator looms large in "authorial novels" without losing his distance from the related events. In contrast, the narrator of a "first-person novel" unmistakably belongs to the fictive world evoked by the story. But the narrator may also "withdraw" from the work to the point of orienting it at the mental vision of one or several of the figures, and then his narration constitutes a "figural novel." [2]

Stanzel keeps his classification commendably supple. Having pointed out that most novels basically rely on one "narrative situation" without avoiding the others altogether, he demonstrates that an exceptional work like James Joyce's *Ulysses* may be based on the approximate balance of all three *Erzählsituationen* (pp. 122ff). Furthermore, Stanzel involves his basic types in a conceptual pattern that allows him to relate intermediate narrative categories to the cardinal points of the system. Thus the "authorial" narrator's cursory remarks in *Vanity Fair* concerning his personal acquaintance with one of the minor characters point toward the integration of the world of the narrator and of "his" figures, that is, toward the situation of the first-person narratives in *Henry Esmond*. Similarly, a distinction between the "narrating self" and the "experiencing self" of first-person narrators helps Stanzel devise an ideal sequence of *Ich-Romane* ranging from almost "authorial" first-person novels (with strong emphasis on the narrator's "narrating self") to interior monologues in which no "narrating self" is present, and this limiting case of the first-person perspective turns into a figural "narrative situation" if the interior monologue assumes the third-person form of substitutionary thought (*erlebte Rede als Gedankendarstellung*).[3] Having discussed intermediate phases between the most typical forms of the "authorial" and the "figural novel" as well, Stanzel interrelates (p. 166) his "narrative situations"

---

[2] I am adopting the three English terms from James P. Pusack's translation of Stanzel's *Narrative Situations in the Novel* (Bloomington, 1971).

[3] Cf. Appendix: "Free Indirect Discourse and Related Techniques."

and Emil Staiger's "basic attitudes" by means of the accompanying diagram.*

Despite differences in critical method and terminology, Stanzel's types reveal strong affinities with the modes of narration delineated by Percy Lubbock. The "authorial novel" corresponds to the panoramic mode in many respects, and the "first-person novel" practically coincides with the mode of the dramatized narrator. Stanzel's concept of the "figural novel," however, combines (or, rather, fails to distinguish) scenic narration and the evocation of the inner scene of a dramatized consciousness. Stanzel discusses what he calls the objective scene as the "special case" of figural representation in which the point of view is *not* attached to any given figure (p. 23). But this definition is far from being satisfactory. In the first place, it is difficult to see why Stanzel thinks it fit

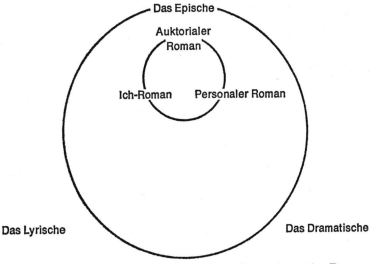

*From F. K. Stanzel, *Die typischen Erzählsituationen im Roman*, Wilhelm Braumüller, Vienna, 1955. Reprinted by permission.

to include what he himself regards as a "neutral" mode of representation in a type of storytelling defined precisely with respect to its reliance on a "figural" perspective. Secondly, Stanzel admits that vividly described conversational scenes in the mode of neutral representation often occur in the context of authorial narration (p. 28), and it should be added that their occurrence is by no means exceptional in "first-person novels" either. Thus I am inclined to suspect that the attraction of the number three for generic critics has induced Stanzel to subsume the "neutral," in fact *inter*personal, mode under the general heading of "figural representation" (*personale Darstellung*). For, as can be seen in the above diagram, Stanzel regards the authorial, first-person, and figural types of the novel as suggestive, on a larger scale, of three genres or attitudes of literature—the epic, the lyric, and the dramatic.

In a penetrating article entitled "Point of View in Fiction: The Development of a Critical Concept" (1955), Norman Friedman describes eight narrative modes in a sequence proceeding "from the one extreme to the other: from statement to inference, from exposition to presentation, from narrative to drama, from explicit to implicit, from idea to image" (p. 1169). Closest to the pole of "telling" is the mode of *Editorial Omniscience*, "the free verse of fiction," providing the narrator with unlimited (and often abused) freedom to choose any verbal channel of information through which to convey any aspect of the story (p. 1180). Next comes the mode of *Neutral Omniscience* in which the narrator's superior and explanatory tone prevails without such overt intrusions into the characters' fictive world as thematic meditations or direct addresses to the reader. But the narrator may leave his stance outside the story altogether, and as he moves from the periphery toward the center of the plot he will speak, first, in the mode of the *Witness-Narrator* and, at last, in the mode of the *Protagonist Narrator*. In stories for which the narrator's insight into brains is more important than his motivated proximity to the fields of action, an apparent recourse to omniscience may be in order. Yet the mode of *Selective Omniscience* differs from all four previously described modes in its narrator's avoidance of retrospective summary: he shows us "thought, perceptions, and feelings as they occur consecutively and in detail passing through the mind" of one or, in the case of *Multiple Selective Omniscience*, several of the characters (p. 1176). Any further approach to the pole of "showing" must forego, Friedman argues, the direct presentation of mental states. The *Dramatic Mode* with its tight-lipped rendition of dialogue and action can at best make readers infer what a more outspoken narrator might "tell" or "show" them about a human consciousness, and the same holds for Friedman's mode of *The Camera*—the first-person account of an uninterrupted stream of experience. Based on the narrow ground of the first episode in Christopher Isherwood's *Goodbye to Berlin* (1939), Friedman's concept of the literary camera fails to encompass the entire field of the interior monologue; as the most consistent early employment of this narrative technique, Arthur Schnitzler's "Leutnant Gustl" (1901) may serve to demonstrate that the writer's "camera" need not keep its shutters closed to the "inner scene" of the ostensible speaker's mind. Still, not even the most recent developments in the area of the *nouveau roman* invalidate Friedman's general remarks about *The Camera* as "the ultimate in authorial exclusion" to be achieved in literature. Being "a process of abstraction, selection, omission, and arrangement," the very act of writing frustrates all attempts undertaken by verbal means at capturing the concrete, unin-

terrupted fullness of any—be it physical, be it psychic—
reality (pp. 1178f).

This last point is argued at greater length in Wayne C.
Booth's *Rhetoric of Fiction* (1961). Challenging the "gross
imprecision" involved in the distinction between biased "telling" and objective "showing," Booth insists that the author's
judgment is always evident "to anyone who knows how to
look for it." Since the writer may choose his disguises but
cannot choose to disappear, he must strive to create an image
of himself which "his most intelligent and perceptive readers" will be able to admire (pp. 20, 154f, 395). Booth, of
course, does not identify the authorial image, more or less
overtly implied in all literary works, with the actual personality of the writer. He discusses various degrees of the narrator's "reliability" as resulting from the presence or absence
of tensions between the narrator and the implied—not the
actual—author in a given work of fiction (pp. 158f). Booth
seems fully justified in arguing that the image of the implied
author must unmistakably emerge from a novel if the reader
is to know just how fallible or trustworthy the narrator's intellectual and moral judgments are. But I cannot share his
general objections to works in which the narrator's reliability
is ambiguous rather than manifestly confirmed or denied
(pp. 396ff *et passim*). The intellectual or even moral purport
of certain works requires that the "implied author" should
himself be, as it were, uncertain about the kind and degree
of the reliability of his narrator(s).

Freed from its narrowly moralistic connotations, Booth's
concept of the implied author seems to me a highly valuable
contribution to literary theory at large. Well beyond the
confines of narrative fiction, such a concept may help to
clarify the necessary distinction between "mimetic" and

"thematic" aspects of literature. As Robert Humphrey (1954), Melvin Friedman (1955), and other students of the stream-of-consciousness novel have pointed out, writers tend to impose elaborate "poetic" patterns of images and symbols on what they present as ostensibly free associations of a character's ruminating mind. This type of "authorial interference" serves a double purpose. On the one hand, it helps to evoke an imaginative world coherent enough for the reader to contemplate. On the other, it "implies" an author who sees the world as consisting of a given set of patterns. Clearly, the implied author must corroborate, contradict, or qualify what each of his speakers says *and yet say nothing* lest he himself turn into just another speaker whose reliability might be questioned. The implied author thus communicates in and through the work as a whole—not in individual "lyric passages" or in direct appeals to the reader (those are "spoken" by the narrator). Whenever an unformulated theme shines through the verbal medium or the imaginative world of a work we see the implied author, that is to say, the thematic rather than the mimetic principle of literature at work. Of the constant interaction between the two principles in every genuine instance of verbal art more will be said in my Conclusions and Propositions.

Along with a considerable number of other critics, those cited in the last few pages have elucidated some "lyric"—or perhaps rather thematic—and many "dramatic" aspects of narrative fiction. Less systematic attention has been devoted to the nature of nondramatic aspects in dramatic literature. Most critics before as well as after the publication of Joyce's *Portrait* (1916) could have readily endorsed Stephen Dedalus's suggestive description of dramatic form: "the artist, like the God of the creation, remains within or behind or beyond or above his handiwork, invisible, refined out of existence, paring his fingernails" (p. 252). Yet this image of an absent deity does better justice to the director's role in individual performances than to the playwright's concrete ubiquity in the text of his drama.

As Roman Ingarden argued in *Das literarische Kunstwerk* (1931), the utterances of a dramatic figure manifest his state of mind only because they are designated as spoken words uttered by that particular figure. Thus the "side text" (*Nebentext*) in which the playwright indicates by whom, where, when, and how the words of the "main text" (*Haupttext*) of his work are uttered permeates the dialogue, as it were, with invisible quotation marks (p. 220). To be sure, the subsidiary function of the "side text" often reduces its author to the stylistic level of an actor or stage director adding explanatory remarks to a part. Hence the partially justified trend in drama criticism to regard the text of plays as a mere point of departure for the craft and imagination of the performing artists. Yet dramatic texts have been read even while their theatrical reproduction was neither feasible nor desired. Ingarden's comments on the "nondramatic" ingredients of printed plays are, therefore, highly relevant to the study of the verbal structure of drama. Furthermore, the very dialogue of great dramatic works exhibits significant deviations from the prevailing theoretical concept of drama as a strictly figural text with the author "refined out of existence, paring his fingernails."

An important chapter in Una Ellis-Fermor's *Frontiers of Drama* (1945) highlights such a deviation: "The Revelation of Unspoken Thought in Drama." Mrs. Ellis-Fermor contrasts scope and style of the naturalistic dialogue to more liberal views of what can be rendered in the form of the characters' speech: "There is a continual struggle to maintain such effect of actuality as is necessary for conviction, upon the one hand, and to convey to the audience, on the other, more knowledge of the issues of the play than strict verisimilitude will allow" (pp. 125f). In the strategy of that perennial struggle Mrs. Ellis-Fermor assigns great importance to the chorus in Greek, and to the soliloquy in Elizabethan drama. The stylistic principles underlying these two conventions are, of course, far from being identical. In Shakespeare's monologues we are listening "not to the most direct presentation that art can make, but to something at one remove from this"; instead of the *direct speech* of the characters the Elizabethan monologue renders their *direct thought* —a kind of communication "more nearly akin to narrative or lyric" than to the usual form of communication in "strict drama" (p. 107). the same antinaturalistic tendency is even more noticeable in the function of the chorus which, at further remove from "direct presentation," contributes to Greek tragedy "a body of common thought and feeling without which the dialogue would be bleak and limited, yet which the main actors in those circumstances could never utter themselves" (p. 102). In other words, the dramatic chorus helps the implied author qualify—not state or interpret—the meaning of the main characters' deeds and speeches.

Perhaps because Bertolt Brecht, the most influential recent German playwright, liked to propagate the dramaturgical principles of his "epic theater" as particularly up to date, several German critics have focused their search for seemingly nondramatic aspects of drama on modern plays. Most important of all, Peter Szondi devoted his *Theorie des modernen Dramas* (1956) to late nineteenth- and twentieth-century departures from "strict drama" in lyric as well as narrative directions. Szondi's concept of drama proper relies on what he describes as the Renaissance persuasion that human beings fully manifest themselves in and through their interaction with other human beings. Szondi argues that the most adequate way to represent such a self-reliant breed of men is by means of dialogue—the "absolute" form in which the "ever present interpersonal action" does not appear dependent on the vast dimensions of past and future time, on a narrator's exterior or one character's interior perspective, nor else on some social or private condition inevitably determining the course of events (pp. 12, 62). Szondi believes that since the last decades of the nineteenth century we tend to experience time as a subjective interpenetration of past, present, and future, and to entertain serious doubts as to whether human deeds spring from free will and lend themselves to intersubjective evaluation. Hence the discrepancy, as Szondi argues, between traditional form and new content—between intersubjective dialogue on the one hand and "objective" or "subjective" aspects of life on the other—in some works of Ibsen, Strindberg, Chekhov, Maeterlinck, and the early Gerhart Hauptmann. It is this very discrepancy that the dramaturgical innovations of Pirandello, O'Neill, Brecht, Wilder, and some other twentieth-century playwrights undertake to abolish. Interpreting the innovations as attempts to find suitable dramatic forms for new (and in the old sense radically antidramatic) contents, Szondi sketches a thought-provoking theory of "stylistic change" with the dialectical phases of harmony (thesis), opposition (antithesis), and reconciliation (synthesis) between theme and structure (pp. 65ff).

It is unfortunate that Szondi slights or overlooks the continuous tradition of "irregular" drama between the Renaissance and the turn of our century. In contrast, Volker Klotz's detailed comparative treatment of *Geschlossene und offene Form im Drama* (1960) delineates two types of dramatic structure without dogmatically associating them with distinct periods of history. Adapting the art critic Heinrich Wölfflin's *Kunstgeschichtliche Grundbegriffe* (1915) to the needs of literary theory, Klotz distinguishes the closed form of (mainly French classical) drama presenting a unified "section as one whole" from the open form attempting to encompass "the whole in sections." Of his systematic analyses of the action, time, space, characters, language, and composition in some thirty (mostly German) plays, the distinction between two ways of treating time seems to me especially original. Whereas the uninterrupted flow of causally interwoven moments "swallows" the unique temporal quality of individual scenes in the closed form of neoclassical and "well-made" plays, open drama (Georg Büchner's, for instance) will sacrifice the sense of temporal continuity in order to explore each of a series of loosely connected scenes as an experienced "moment" (*Augenblick*) (p. 232). It may be well to point out that such a "deviation" from the even flow and intersubjective temporal perspective of "dramatic action" prevails in the verbal structure of a good deal of Greek, Elizabethan, and modern "open drama."

As for lyric poetry, I am not aware of any widely shared concept of its generic structure. While deep insights have been attained with regard to certain kinds of *non*-dramatic, *non*-narrative writing, critics do not seem to have succeeded in providing a unified conceptual map of this "no man's land." Perhaps they ought to quit trying; this is at least what René Wellek suggests in a recent article on "Genre Theory, the Lyric, and *Erlebnis*" (1967). Wellek is particularly skeptical about German discussions of "the lyric" in such terms as subjective experience (*Erlebnis*) and mood (*Stimmung*). He points out that "the supposed intensity, inwardness, immediacy of an experience can never be demonstrated as certain and can never be shown as relevant to the quality of art." But Wellek makes clear that his criticism is not limited to the "expressive" notions of what lyric poetry at large is or should be. While acknowledging the usefulness of such concepts as the song, the elegy, or the ode, he opposes all efforts to evolve a unified theory of lyric poetry. In Wellek's opinion, "one must abandon attempts to define the general nature of the lyric" and turn "to the history and thus the description of genres which can be grasped in their concrete conventions and traditions" (pp. 251f). Wellek's dissatisfaction with existing concepts of the lyric seems justified. Yet future theories may disprove the unfavorable prognosis his argument implies. There are encouraging signs in many twentieth-century pronouncements on three apparent dichotomies which would need to be reconciled by any new "structural" theory of lyric literature: dichotomies of prosody (prose *versus* verse), diction (elaboration *versus* simplicity) and truthfulness (palpable stylization *versus* suggested sincerity).

Mindful of the conclusions reached in the pertinent discussions of the latter part of the eighteenth century, modern critics refuse to base their concept of the lyric on prosodic criteria. It was not only "free verse" like Walt Whitman's that proved to be compatible with our idea of poetry. In his article "Über zeitliche Perspektive in der neueren französichen Literatur" (1923), Leo Spitzer could without much ado subscribe to the "well-known dictum" praising prose writers as the greatest preromantic *poets* of France (pp. 263f); and

Roman Jakobson exemplified his concept of the lyric as the genre of "the first person and the present time" with reference to Boris Pasternak's short stories and autobiography. (Cf. "Randbemerkungen zur Prosa des Dichters Pasternak," 1935).

There is, of course, much less agreement as far as the salient characteristics of lyric *diction* are concerned. In fact two schools, each of which largely ignores the other, seem to hold disparate views on the subject. Folk poetry, and especially the congenial use that Goethe and some later Romanticists made of its rhetorical devices, have so impressed many German critics that they consider "pure" lyric poetry as a kind of artless, spontaneous singing—in Wordsworth's truncated phrase, the "overflow of powerful feelings," not their recollection "in tranquillity." At the opposite extreme we have some English and American critics whose excessive concern for complex ambiguities and ironic depths presupposes, both in the writer's and the reader's mind, a kind of tranquillity too impervious to give way (as Wordsworth also demands) to an esthetic emotion "kindred to" personal feelings. But the best critics—whether "old" or "new"— embrace concepts of the lyric which are not mutually exclusive. Although firmly rooted in the German tradition, Oskar Walzel pointed out as early as 1916 that the "object" (*Gegenstand*) of genuine lyric poetry is not subjective experience but "something universal and ever-recurring that has completely detached itself from the poet's personality" (p. 270). In turn Cleanth Brooks, perhaps the most representative New Critic, suggests that "even metaphor," by asserting an identification that is literal nonsense, "directs attention to the situation, to the character of the speaker, and the occasion." (Cf. Wimsatt and Brooks, *Literary Criticism*, p. 676.) Clearly enough, metaphor and some other devices of what Brooks elsewhere described as poetry's "Language of Paradox" can help complex poems to evoke the image of the speaker as the implied author's reliable spokesman. The vividness of this image will, of course, depend on what the Russian Formalists called the "speech orientation" (*rechevaja ustanovka*) of different poetic genres: whether the given poem is "geared" to oratory, conversation, singing, or any other "level of non-literary discourse." (Cf. Erlich, *Russian Formalism*, p. 204.) Indeed, Roland Barthes's view that modern poetry ostensibly renounces the social function of language seems to be based on the fact that the radical symbolism of Rimbaud, Mallarmé, and their followers does not suggest a direct analogy to any kind of nonliterary use of words. Still, if such poems suppress (as they often do) the image of the "speaker," they make the selective craftmanship of an implied author stand all the more conspicuously to the eye; and the image of this implied author permeates the "existential geology" of multiple meanings which Barthes discerns under each word of seemingly uncommunicative literary texts. (Cf. Barthes, *Le Degré zéro de l'écriture*, pp. 68ff.)

Whether a vividly evoked speaker, a forcefully implied author, or the complete integration of both, a single "meaner" emerges from the monological structure of most lyric poems. This, of course, should not induce the critic to try his hand at reconstructing the "real" personality of the writer. Attempts at tracing a poem back to its psychological source distract us from the poem by directing attention, in T. S. Eliot's words, "on to something else which, in the form in which it can be apprehended by the critic and his readers, has no relation to the poem and throws no light upon it" (*The Three Voices of Poetry*, p. 31). Kenneth Burke may be justified in arguing that most poets prefer certain types of masks to playing, as it were, "repertory theater" (*The Philosophy of Literary Form*, p. 18). Yet the poet's sincerity, that is, the kind and degree of correspondence between his actual character and his image (implied by his favorite "masks") has no esthetic relevance whatsoever. For the casual reader the convincing appearance of sincerity suffices, and the best structural critics know that their job is completed when they have accounted for the verbal means through which that appearance had been successfully evoked.

2. *Mimetic Concepts*

The concepts of genre to be discussed in the remaining part of this chapter focus on similarities between the worlds different literary works evoke. Few modern critics regard the world of a work as the "imitation" of something external to it. Indeed, the original connotations of the Greek word point to "representation" as a better translation of *mimesis*. Such a rendering of his pivotal concept permits the mimetic critic to relate the world of a work—its plot, characters, and general atmosphere—to life outside literature without postulating, as did Socrates in the tenth book of Plato's *Republic*, a purely derivative connection between art and reality. Since 1555 at the very latest, critics such as Hieronymus Fracastoro would even argue that the poet discloses something like Platonic ideas—the perfected image of nature.

Convinced that art "unfolds truth" rather than produces "playthings," Georg Wilhelm Friedrich Hegel was deeply concerned with distinguishing various ways in which different literary genres convey different aspects of esthetic truth. In his posthumously published *Vorlesungen über die Ästhetik* (1835), Hegel discussed epic poetry as the chief vehicle of objective revelations about man's exterior universe, lyric poems as subjective disclosures of the inner world of particularized individuals, and drama as the synthesis of the epic principle and the lyric: the playwright objectifies his characters' particular subjectivities in dramatic dialogue and action. This dialectical tripartition of literature had been foreshadowed by Novalis, Schelling, and the Schlegel brothers, and was to become embalmed and canonized in Friedrich Theodor Vischer's bulky *Ästhetik* (1846–1857). Small wonder that most German critics in the mimetic tradition have rather accepted or somewhat modified than ignored or altogether rejected the time-honored association of genres with an objective, a subjective, and a "synthetic" mode of mimesis.

In *Das Stilgesetz der Poesie* (1901), Th. A. Meyer attempted to qualify the concepts "objective" and "subjective" in terms of literary imagery. In keeping with his view of language as the "marvelous abbreviation of reality," Meyer insists that it is merely the appearance (*Schein*) of objectivity which the epic poet's sensuously detailed descriptions create. To be sure, the leisurely progress of epic narrative tends to suggest that the writer has subdued his subjectivity by completely devoting himself to his story. Yet it is only by comparison to the even more allusive and fragmentary nature of lyric and dramatic imagery that narrative discourse would seem to be an "objective" representation of reality. While the lyric poet and the playwright tend to evoke inner worlds with a bare minimum of concern for outward reality, the narrative writer will linger over sensuous details without surpassing the inherent limitations of language—its failure to encompass the totality of simultaneous and continuous existence in an unmediated (and thus "objective") manner (p. 196).

In *Die Rolle des Erzählers in der Epik* (1910), Käte Friedemann reconsidered the concept of epic objectivity from
another point of view. Flaubert's German contemporaries
(and among them most notably the talented critic and
novelist Friedrich Spielhagen) had connected the romantic
ideal of epic objectivity with the demand for a predominantly
"scenic," impersonal, matter-of-fact style in narrative fiction.
Refusing to expose narrative works to the standards of what
she calls "dramatic illusion," Käte Friedemann defends the
palpable presence of the narrator in the world of a novel
against Spielhagen's theoretical campaign. She argues that
precisely the author's overt treatment of his plot and characters as fictive displays a truly superior attitude of "intellectual objectivity." In Käte Friedemann's mimetic view, one
function of the storyteller in narrative works is to manifest
the "dual nature of everything that is and happens" (*Doppel-
natur alles Geschehens*): placing apparently self-sufficient
entities in the context of his narration, he succeeds in intimating that they are really parts of a whole (pp. 5f, 221).

Ernst Hirt's *Formgesetz der epischen, dramatischen und
lyrischen Dichtung* (1923) shed new light on how the narrative perspective can reveal the "dual nature" of the world.
According to Hirt's adaptation of the old metaphor likening
the progress of time to the flux of a river, "the epic poet
beholds the current of Becoming from a distance." As he
does not limit his work to a mere account of what he "sees"
(that is: the events and characters of his story) but voices his
"personal" opinion about it, he blends Being and Becoming.
This argument commends itself by pointing beyond the abstract norm of "epic objectivity"—the supposedly total
exclusion of the writer's personality from the world of his
imagination. Even with regard to the "purest" narrative

genre, the great epic poem, Hirt explicitly qualifies the norm: authorial interference is avoided "theoretically," or "as far as language permits" (pp. 51, 217). On this view, narrative literature appears to hold a "synthetic" central position between "subjective" lyric and fully "objective" drama because it interrelates subject (the narrator) and object (the story). Such a scheme—first sketched by Friedrich Schlegel (1797) but also adopted by Jean Paul Richter and Schopenhauer in the early decades of the nineteenth century—does better justice to the worlds evoked by literary works than the rather dogmatic interpretation of a historical sequence—Homer, the ancient Greek lyric poets, Periclean drama—in the dialectical terms of objective thesis, subjective antithesis, and dramatic synthesis.

Henri Bonnet, of course, need not worry about reconciling the epic poet's and the playwright's conflicting claims to objectivity. In *Roman et poésie: Essai sur l'esthétique des genres* (1951), he argues that drama is merely a "formal genre," equally suitable as a vehicle for "novelistic or poetic substance" (p. 122). In Bonnet's opinion, beauty is a form of truth (p. 12), and art is a mode of knoweldge (p. 16). Novel and poetry are the only fundamental genres of literature, representing extreme possibilities of its cognitive function; whereas science aims at measurable quantities, novels afford objective, poems subjective, insights into qualitative aspects of human life. Yet the two major genres of literature are not completely divorced from the other arts, science, and philosophy. Bonnet aligns the bulk of representative painting and sculpture with objective *roman;* architecture, music, and arabesque, with subjective *poésie;* dance will lean toward one or the other according to its primary concern for imitation or stylization. He further suggests that the novel can move toward sociology and psychology through the intermediate field of "moralistic character portray" (*caractérologie moraliste*). "Pure poetry" in turn appears on Bonnet's conceptual map of human consciousness as an area adjacent to metaphysics (p. 241 *et passim*).

The idea of a dialectical correlation between subjective and objective components pervades Theodor W. Adorno's concepts of narrative as well as lyric literature. In an essay "Über epische Naivetät" (1943, first published in 1958), Adorno links the epic breadth of Homer to the active interest Goethe, Adalbert Stifter, and Gottfried Keller took in painting as related attempts of writers to emancipate artistic representation from the rule of "subjective reason" informing verbal discourse. Of the two kinds of endeavor, Homer's was "desperate," for, using language as a means of representation, the verbal artist cannot avoid a certain "conceptual manipulation of things" (pp. 55f). In a later study of the "Standort des Erzählers im zeitgenössischen Roman" (1954), Adorno considers the inevitable manipulation not of things through language, but of human beings in industrial societies, and the impress of this manipulation on contemporary novel writing. The two essays supplement each other in suggesting five historical phases of the seesaw between the "objective" and the "subjective" principle of narration. On the one hand, Homer's seemingly unselective, "naive" concern for details, Flaubert's conscious care for the illusion of impartiality, and Joyce's objectified recording of the stream of a consciousness represent the most conspicuous instances of three types of "objective" storytelling. On the other, Adorno distinguishes two reasons for which "subjective" narrators would intrude into the world of their story. Before Flaubert, such an intrusion served as the overtly moralizing part of characterization.

After him, and especially with Thomas Mann, the intrusion
tends to result from the writer's ironic partisanship "against
the lie of representation"—the false appearance of objectivity;
thus it is ultimately directed "against the narrator himself"
(pp. 67ff).

Adorno's "Rede über Lyrik und Gesellschaft" (1957)
concentrates on the "collective undercurrent" abiding in great
lyric poems despite the poets' "subjective" surface motivation. According to Adorno, the lyric poet's self-expression
voices a protest against alienation on behalf of those who do
not share his privilege of leisure and education and who
would therefore strive in vain to grasp "objective" universals
in a consistently "subjective" process of introversion. Furthermore, the lyric identification of an individual's subjectivity with the objective expressive force inherent in language triumphs over the double predicament which modern
life imposes upon human beings—their monadistic opposition
to, and their self-alienated functioning within, social mechan-
isms (pp. 86ff).

In his Marburg lecture *Über die Elemente der Poesie und
den Begriff des Dramatischen* (1903), Ernst Elster had abandoned the most influential German estheticians' threefold
classification of literature. Still, his distinction between "objective" and "subjective contents" clearly presupposes the
dichotomy of *Ich* and *Nicht-Ich*, the self and the world,
underlying the generic concepts of Schelling, Hegel, and
Vischer. Elster argues that the processes of life (to be *narrated*) and its conditions as well as diverse objects and their
qualities (to be *described*) constitute the "objective contents
of literature" while the "subjective contents" emerge as the

poet's *emotive* or *meditative* reactions to those "objective contents." Thus the narrative, descriptive, lyric, and meditative "elements of literature" seem at first sight to exhaust the realm of possible contents. Yet Elster adds drama as the fifth "element" which, a mere form of discourse at the outset, has gradually embraced volitive action as its own adequate generic content (pp. 5, 9f). Elster's best observations transcend the limits of his pseudoscientific concept of literary *element*. Most notably, he concedes that the five "elements" of literature often manifest themselves in and through each other. Narration can enliven contents normally associated with description (indeed, Lessing's *Laokoon* urged that it ought to do so); the meditative element may be embodied in dramatic action, narration, description, or "lyric outbursts"; and a lyric mood can emanate from narrative, dramatic, meditative, or descriptive modes of discourse. Allowing any "element" of literature to supplement the mimetic function of any other, Elster's concept of genre implies—although it surely falls far short of formulating—a necessary distinction between the world that emerges from a literary work and the way in which the work evokes this world.

The Polish critic Juliusz Kleiner based the following classification on his study of "The Role of Time in Literary Genres" (1926):

A. Poetry of spatial relations or descriptive poetry
B. Poetry of defined time
   1. Poetry of the past or epics
   2. Poetry of the present or lyrics
   3. Poetry aimed at the future or drama
C. Poetry of all times or didactic poems
D. Extratemporal poetry or tales

In contrast to other followers of Jean Paul Richter's and Friedrich Theodor Vischer's influential association of the lyric with the present, the epic with the past, and drama with the future, Kleiner does not wish to connect every work of literature to one or more of the three "dimensions" of time. He can discuss the three familiar genres of "defined time" without having to claim that their principles of composition exhaust the entire realm of literary technique; his distinctions between the dramatic *unity* of endeavor, the lyric *unity* of experience and the looser narrative treatment of the *relations* between reminiscences classify only the center and not the whole of literature (pp. 10f).

To be sure, Kleiner holds the mimetic view that "poetry is strictly associated with the perception of life." From this and from his second premise according to which "life cannot be described without the frame of the moving stream of time," he can plausibly conclude that some reference to concrete time is needful for works to qualify as "undoubtedly poetic." As a result, the three genres accounting for time in the concrete often lend their "characteristic form" to other kinds of works. For instance, whenever the subject matter of a literary piece has the nature of an occurrence, the narrative form of the epic will have to be employed, even though the didactic poem or fairy tale in question may have very little in common with facts of the past. As a result, tales may seem to look back to a beloved past. Actually, however, "they are controlled by desires and not by reminiscences"; "in spirit," therefore, tales are oriented toward the future (pp. 6, 12). Distinguishing the narrative "form" from the dramatic "spirit" of tales, Kleiner approaches a theoretical stance from which one can see the world of a literary work as relying on, yet distinct from, the verbal artifact which is capable of evoking it in a reader's mind.

André Jolles's radical departure from the tradition of tripartite classifications takes us further away from such a stance. Jolles describes nine *Einfache Formen* (1930) as morphological archetypes of literary works. Each of the Simple Forms—legend, saga, myth, riddle, adage, test case, anecdote, fairy tale, and the laughable—springs from a specific "intellectual orientation" (*Geistesbeschäftigung*) which selects and orders aspects of the world according to its own pattern. Transforming "processes of life" into "verbal gestures" (*Sprachgebärden*), the Simple Forms enter oral literature as Realized Simple Forms (*Gegenwärtige Einfache Formen*). The legend of Saint George, for example, realizes potentialities of the underlying Simple Form concerned with exemplary human behavior, and the proverb "Lügen haben kurze Beine" makes use of the compressive power of adage (*Spruch*): "lies have short legs" (and thus cannot escape being caught) summarizes a certain range of experience without recourse to abstract thinking. The more complex works of written literature are at further remove from the Simple Forms but still rely on one of the nine kinds of "intellectual orientation" and evoke a world by means of "verbal gestures" characteristic of a particular Simple Form. Unfortunately, Jolles describes some types of "intellectual orientation" in terms of their target, others in terms of their function; for instance, concern for tribe and family characterizes the orientation underlying saga, but its efficacy in yielding essential knowledge defines the orientation constitutive of myth (pp. 17f, 220, *et passim*).

Similar incoherence impairs the exposition of Jolles's central concept of "verbal gesture." Regarding works of literature as natural organisms brought into existence by some creative power inherent in language, Jolles fails to distinguish between the truly verbal aspect and the imaginative world of literary works. As a result, his concept of "verbal gesture" confounds motifs of mimesis with traits of style. To cite two extreme cases, such motifs as "a wheel with sharp blades" or "an idol that bursts" pass for the verbal gestures of legend while the esoterically ambiguous use of words is presented as the characteristic verbal gesture of riddle (*Rätsel*). Even the illuminating comparison between the salient features of fairy tale (*Märchen*) and those of the realistic short story stemming from anecdote (*Memorabile*) disappoints whenever the concept of "verbal gesture" occurs in it. Understandably enough; for Jolles's distinction between the pertinent intellectual orientations—the desire to transcend the amoral frame of reality on the one hand, the interest in concrete details of a specific event on the other—delineates two different *types of world* largely independent of the *modes of evoking a world* by means of languages.

Despite its vague concepts, extravagant terminology, and excessive pretensions, Jolles's study has considerable merit as a mimetic theory of genre. First, it sharpens its readers awareness of the variety of (not necessarily nine) distinct types of worlds that emerge from literary works. Next, by distinguishing Simple Forms from Realized Simple Forms and more complex Artistic Forms (*Kunstformen*), Jolles stresses the important difference between the types of worlds literary works *can* evoke, and the individual world every one of them *does* evoke, by means of words. Finally, even though his neo-Romantic concept of "creative language" seems out of alignment with the actual formation of the works of written as well as oral literature, it may yield certain insights since the nature of language indeed predetermines, if not the nature of imaginative worlds, the modes of their verbal evocation.

In contrast to Jolles's radically innovative classification, many modern critics distinguish opposed types of imaginative worlds in the framework of the time-honored dichotomy tragedy *versus* comedy. Some will suggest slight modifications of those traditional concepts without regard for wide applicability. Others purport rather comprehensive new systems ignoring the primary purpose of genre studies—the promotion of the understanding of a given group of literary works. But interest in concrete works and concern for significant range in validity can be kept in balance, and such a balance was achieved in at least two recent American critics' explorations of the tragic and the comic as interrelated phenomena.

In ten lucid papers, published or orally delivered from 1935 on and posthumously collected in *Tragedy: A View of Life* (1956), Henry Alonzo Myers made a remarkably good case for a theory which at first glance may seem far too moralistic. Myers argues that our delight in tragic spectacles of evil and suffering stems from tragedy's revelation of "significant patterns" in the apparent chaos of human experience. Tragic works demonstrate "that character is fate and that men are united in the justice which apportions equal measures of joy and sorrow to each individual" (p. 123). This tragic sense of a just order in the moral universe need not be voiced on the extreme pitch of drama revealing how "the hero takes all, gives all, in one grand moment" (p. 149). The fact that "men pay with their lives for experience" can also be seen in works suggesting that the moderate man loses in intensity what he gains in terms of duration—the number of years he is likely to live.

Whether or not written in the form of dialogue, works focusing on the everyday life of moderate men are seldom "dramatic," as they tend to lack intensity, suspense, surprise, reversal, and other dramatic qualities. Conversely, a heroic singleness of purpose in the main character easily turns a novel like *Moby Dick* into "drama" in Myers's sense of the word. Drama thus requires unyielding heroes ready to pay any price for the attainment of their goals. Yet Myers also insists that the uncompromising, "monomaniac" hero's fate is different from his fellowmen's in degree rather than in kind. "The great turn of the wheel of fortune which carries the hero to the extremes of joy and grief, often in one moment of dazzling intensity, is the dramatic symbol of the endless little ups and downs, the little sorrows and joys, of ordinary men" (pp. 138ff). In other words, drama does not falsify or distort life; it projects certain elements in life to a larger, more visible screen.

Myers supplies a large number of illustrations for his basic tenet according to which tragedy demonstrates that "man can get what he wants—if he is willing to pay the price": "Oedipus finds the unknown murderer; Orestes and Hamlet punish the murderers of their fathers; Medea crushes Jason; Tamburlaine conquers kingdoms and empires; Doctor Faustus has his four and twenty years, and Faust his fair moment; Romeo is united with Juliet in life and in death; Lear has ample proof of Cordelia's love, as does Othello of Desdemona's; Everyman is saved; Samson destroys the Philistines; Solness climbs the tower; Ahab hurls the harpoon at Moby

Dick." The price to be paid is usually the hero's life, and his death is almost always preceded by moments (or years) of life worse than death. Yet, Myers argues, "tragedy is not a spectacle of futility and frustration; it is the demonstration of the universal moral law: man gets what he pays for, and pays for what he gets" (p. 157).

Naturally, Myers knows that his postulated equation of joy and sorrow is not always self-evident—not, at least, within the confines of our day-to-day existence. Hence the great significance of comedy: it "reconciles us through laughter to the disorder, the nonsense, the incongruities and absurdities which we meet everywhere in experience" (p. 123). Representing his characters with detachment rather than empathy, the comic poet makes his reader see them from the outside, as it were, rather than from within. As a result, the "tragic" questions whether character determines fate and whether a given character suffers and enjoys in equal measure will not demand to be answered. Myers distinguishes two kinds of comic heroes: those treated in good humor and those turned into butts for satire. But the glory of all comedy lies for him in the "transformation of the frustrations of reason into soothing laughter" (pp. 114, 126).

Myers is critical of Horace Walpole's famous dictum that "the world is a comedy to those that think, a tragedy to those that feel." Albert Cook in turn selects a French proverb very much to the same effect as one of the mottoes for *The Dark Voyage and the Golden Mean: A Philosophy of Comedy* (1949): "Qui sent, pleurt; qui pense, rit" (p. 29). The juxtaposition of feeling and thought is, however, not central to Cook's variations on the following theme: tragedy and comedy see (and show) the world under the aspect of the Wonderful and the Probable, respectively. Despite their radically different orientations, the tragic and the comic writer need not be unduly selective in finding appropriate topics for one or the other "symbolic attitude." In a sense each achieves his goal contrary to expectations: "Where comedy says, 'even in the nonprobable does the predictable take place,' tragedy says, 'even in the probable, the wonderful is manifest' " (p. 44).

Like Myers, Cook conceives of the two genres broadly. Tragedy and comedy are not necessarily written in the dialogue form of drama: *The Odyssey*, *Don Quixote*, *Tom Jones*, and *Finnegans Wake* are among Cook's discussed samples of comedy. Nor does the happy or unhappy outcome of an action determine whether it be classified as tragic or comic: "*Philoctetes* and *The Tempest* are both profound, and both have a happy ending; one is tragedy, the other comedy" (p. 32). What, then, makes the difference? In accordance with his wonderful-probable dichotomy, Cook contrasts tragedy's reliance on ultimate values (good and evil) to comedy's preoccupation with manners, tragedy's exploration of individual souls to comedy's interest in social contexts (generation, family), tragedy's emphasis on the godlike in man to comedy's stress on qualities men share with beasts and machines (pp. 33ff, 46f). As to the anthropological roots of the two genres, Cook alludes to pagan as well as Christian myths of the "hanged god" on the one hand, and to licentious fertility rites on the other. These religious analogues—or perhaps prototypes—of tragic and comic literature may shed useful light on two juxtaposed trends in relating the main character of a literary work to his fellow human beings. The tragic hero is usually cast out by his norm-abiding society as unclassifiably abnormal, too "far out" for the best social policy of the golden mean. In contrast, most comic characters in a sense reinforce accepted norms by being such laughably "typical norms of abnormality" as the country bumpkin, the boaster, the foreigner, the miser, or the misanthrope (pp. 38f, 43).

In the realm of stage conventions, the tragic soliloquy (character addressing his own soul) corresponds to the comic aside(character addressing the audience). Cook points out that the asides of stage plays manifest a general tendency inherent in comic works of fiction as well as drama: the deliberate breaking of the reader's or spectator's illusion as to the "reality" of the imaginative world he is invited to contemplate. Tragic works, by contrast, require that we take them "seriously" so that we shall "identify ourselves as individuals with the protagonist—whence our pity and terror" (p. 45). Here again the introvert spirit of soulful tragedy emerges as the opposite of the detached skepticism of commonsense comedy. "Le rire, dans la rue; les pleurs, à la maison." As this second French proverb (another one of Cook's many well-chosen mottoes) indicates, folk wisdom may yield insights which somehow eluded many sophisticated dramaturgists, until Henri Bergson, in *Le Rire* (1900), stressed the private depth of tragedy and the public spirit of comedy.

Cook's reinterpretation of two traditional antinomies (failure-success and aristocrat-bourgeois) highlights the fundamental difference between his and Myers's concepts of tragedy and comedy (pp. 41f, 47f). In an unintended (or at least unavowed) piece of polemic against Myers's view of tragedy as the demonstration of justice in the human condition, Cook insists that unrequited pain and ultimate failure in our probable world are essential to the dignity of the tragic hero. The "active hybris" of an Oedipus, Brutus, Lear, or Othello is to deny man's limitations; each feels that his individuality cannot be conquered and that therefore, like a god, "he can will the perfection of his own action." Yet the wonderful attempt to achieve godhead is "an attempt at which man must always fail," and the active hybris of the aristocratic hero will soon have to be "cured"—expiated—by passive suffering. The "passive hybris" of the comic hero who is a bourgeois in spirit (if not indeed in social status as well) is different: "He wants to make sure that when he puts a nickel into the slot machine of the cosmos he gets a full nickel's worth, even if he has to pound the machine violently." Cook warns against confusing this "pounding of the machine" with active hybris. Whereas the tragic hero "actively creates his fate," the bourgeois hero in passive hybris warps his personality "for equity in material exchanges" (pp. 87ff).

In view of this stimulating dichotomy one is left wondering why Ibsen's and Strindberg's heroes whom Cook declares guilty of passive rather than active hybris should be considered heroes of tragedy at all. Many of them would much rather seem to be "warped" heroes of a genre Cook's neat antitheses disregard completely: *tragicomedy* (p. 90). Similarly, when Myers discusses the "endless little ups and downs" as the undramatic yet tragic lot of moderate men, he in fact contrasts the uncompromising hero's truly tragic fate to what is better described as a *tragicomic* seesaw of frustration and fulfillment. Myers ignores that the same seesaw, if projected to the "dramatic" scale of extreme joy and grief, does not remain quite the same; under such circumstances, it reveals the frustration of the hero's attempt to escape from fate's unrelenting balance. Witnessing how the hero "takes all, gives all in one grand moment," the spectator of genuine tragedy gains insight not only into what Myers considers justice—the apportioning of equal measures of joy and sorrow to each individual. Rather, tragedy demonstrates the cosmic injustice done to greatness in every man through the "just" frustration of a great man's aspiration.

Reacting against William Empson and the American New Critics' analytical concentration on the language of literary works, a group of scholars affiliated with the University of Chicago had come to stress the primary importance of the world that literary works evoke. Elder Olson's and Ronald S. Crane's essays, reprinted in *Critics and Criticism* (1952), voiced many of the basic precepts to which, in a more or less consistent way, all critics contributing to that volume had been adhering. What seems to me their most important single tenet was argued by Olson: since most modern critics agree that words *function* in poetry, it should be possible to conclude that "words must be subordinate to their functions, for they are selected and arranged with a view to these" (p. 565). Beside reviving the central concepts of the *Poetics*, the Chicago critics often invoke Aristotle's authority to buttress their own generic classifications. It is, therefore, understandable that the designation of these critics by Kenneth Burke as *Neo-Aristotelians* has been widely accepted. Still, the critics concerned as well as their opponents have often pointed out that the Chicago doctrines deviate from the *Poetics* to a considerable extent.

In the field of genre criticism, the main point of divergence stands clearly to the eye. Whereas Aristotle's distinctions according to the objects, means, and manner of mimesis concern the *whole* of literature *as* a mimetic art, the most general classification suggested by the Chicago critics subdivides literature into a *mimetic* and a *didactic* genre. In a didactic work, Olson declares, everything "exists and has its peculiar character in order to enforce the doctrine." Even though the metaphorical action of didactic allegories "bears, to a superficial view, a close resemblance to a plot," in this kind of poetry "the characters very generally represent the subjects, and the incidents the predicates, of the doctrinal proposition." Such subordination of plot to doctrine can be seen, according to Olson, in Dante's *Divina commedia*. Mimetic works, in contrast, are "ordered to a plot"—a system of incidents which is "not, like allegorical action, complete because it completely expresses a given doctrine but because, as action, it resolves those issues out of which it has begun." With excessive emphasis on the assumed discrepancy between didactic doctrine and mimetic plot, Olson insists that speech is truly meaningful in didactic works while mimetic literature employs speech as action. Accordingly, most of what has been regarded as meaning in mimetic works is "not meaning at all, but implications of character, passion, and fortune derived from the interpretation of speech and action." I believe that Olson's meticulous distinction between "speech as meaningful (lexis) and speech as action (praxis)" reveals rather than eliminates the difficulty in neatly separating entire works into a mimetic and a didactic class. "What the poetic character says in the mimetic poem is speech and has meaning; his *saying it* is action, an act of persuading, confessing, commanding, informing, torturing, or what not. His diction may be accounted for in grammatical and lexicographical terms; not so his action" (pp. 54, 65ff, 71). I fail to see why such statements should describe the nature of a character's speech in the *Iliad* more accurately than in the *Divine Comedy*—Olson's chief examples for mimetic and didactic literature, respectively. Much as the meaning of any communication partly depends on the situational context, poetic meaning and plot are interdependent aspects rather than competing or incompatible ingredients of literary works.

In a more stimulating manner, Olson considers the important but largely neglected question of magnitude with regard to different genres. As vast extension precludes that the whole, and extreme minuteness precludes that the parts, of a work be apprehended properly, the ideal magnitude of literary works lies "in a mean between excess of the part and excess of the whole." But the measure of appropriate size is relative to the individual genres "the parts and whole of which impose different burdens upon the memory": a lyric poem and a tragedy may be equally long, yet only the former "too long" to be adequately remembered (p. 559). The reason for this is indirectly stated in Olson's comments on lyric poetry as a mimetic genre. Most lyric poems present "a single character acting in a single closed situation" in which the character's verbal acts must remain "uncomplicated by any other agency." We may infer that such a simple "object of mimesis" does not allow for the interplay of disclosure and concealment on a scale sufficiently large and variegated for sizable works. Yet the "object imitated" in lyric poems is temporal—Olson insists that even a mood is not something static or timeless but, at its shortest, "momentary"—and thus partial concealment and step-by-step disclosure determine the "manner of representation" in lyric poems just as in other kinds of mimetic literature (pp. 72f, 560ff).

The most concrete contribution of the Chicago school to a modern theory of genre can be found, I believe, in Ronald S. Crane's analysis of *Tom Jones* as a novel with a comic plot. In the course of his intricate argument, Crane implicitly interrelates Aristotle's remarks on the objects of mimesis, plot structure, and the "qualitative parts" of tragedy. Any novel or drama, unless constructed on didactic rather than mimetic principles, represents "human beings interacting with one another in ways determined by, and in turn affecting, their moral characters and their states of mind." The plot of such a work is a "completed process of change" with one of the "causal ingredients"—(1) moral character, (2) action, and (3) reasonings, emotions, attitudes—employed as the "synthetizing principle." While the completed process of change affects all three parts, it is primarily a change of either the protagonist's moral character, or his situation, or else his thoughts and feelings. If we recall that Aristotle demanded of the "perfect" tragedy that it should have (1) a basically good man (2) pass from happiness to misery (3) as a consequence of some great error on his part, we are likely to agree that the "three variables" according to which Crane suggests classifying plots are very Aristotelian indeed. These variables are: (1) the general estimate we are induced to form of the hero's *moral character*, as a result of which we wish for him either good or bad fortune at the end; (2) the pleasurable or painful *events that befall* or are likely to befall the hero; and (3) the degree and kind of his actual *responsibility* for what happens to him. Clearly, Crane's discussion is more sophisticated than the insight it is intended to substantiate, namely, that "the plot of *Tom Jones* has a pervasively comic form" (pp. 620ff, 632f).

Crane and, until very recently, Olson seem to have assumed that all mimetic works are either "serious" or "comic"—in less extreme cases "sympathetic" or "antipathetic" (pp. 555, 623). The substitution of "serious" for "tragic" in the familiar dichotomy is remarkable, for it betrays what I think is an unwarranted evaluative prejudice. In *Tragedy and the Theory*

of Drama (1961) Olson expressly avows: "The distinction between the serious and the comic is one of value; of value as
reckoned in terms of benefit and harm." Whereas tragedy
deals with beneficial or harmful things of major consequence,
comedy "grows out of the unimportant." Unlike tragic characters whom we consider "liable to great good or harm, or
capable of doing these," comic figures do not elicit "serious
emotions." Virtues and vices shown in works belonging to the
comic genre are "either not important ones, or ones producing
no very good or bad result, or fantastic exaggerations of which
we remain incredulous" (pp. 160ff).

To be sure, Olson concedes that comedy is "interesting and
diverting" even though "the merely unimportant is generally
uninteresting." Yet his 1961 discussion does not explain what
precisely makes "unimportant" comic works "gay" or "ridicu-
lous" and therefore also interesting. For such an explanation
we must turn to Olson's more recent *Theory of Comedy*
(1969) which, however, is a theory of the punitive, "ridicu-
lous" comedy only. Here the serious and the comic are juxtaposed as *contrary* rather than merely contradictory categories
with a conceptual no man's land—presumably including the
gay—between them. The serious genre of tragedy excites
concern and leads to a catharsis of pity and fear by "arousing
those emotions to their utmost and providing them with their
most perfect objects." In contrast, the nonserious, "worthless"
incidents and characters of comedy preclude emotional identification. Exhibiting the "sheer absurdity" of taking its butts
seriously, comedy brings about "a relaxation, or as Aristotle
would say, *katastasis* of concern" (pp. 13f, 16ff, 36f).

This juxtaposition of tragedy and comedy as the utmost in
excitement and in total relaxation of concern is reminiscent of
Emil Staiger's suggestive observation that comedy answers the

tragic question "What for?" with another question: "What on earth for?" Yet Olson advocates a further distinction between comic laughter and the "laughter of joy" caused by things gay, light-hearted, playful, or childlike. This distinction permits him to propound a "poetics of comedy" with premeditated neglect for *As You Like It, Twelfth Night,* and most other instances of what C. L. Barber discussed as *Shakespeare's Festive Comedy* (1959). There is, of course, considerable difference between the satiric and the "saturnalian" or festive pattern underlying two main versions of the comic. Since, however, the two patterns tend to emerge from comic works in various combinations, Olson's theory, based on the punitive aspect of the genre, must produce half-truths about the essence of comedy. In any event, this theory fails to account for the joyous, festive, gay, and playful elements permeating all but the most bitter, indeed rather tragicomic, manifestations of the comic (pp. 22f, 86ff).

Although Susanne K. Langer's view that "art is creation of forms symbolic of human feeling" might easily have prompted expressive as well as structural considerations, her interrelation of *Feeling and Form* (1953) evolves primarily along mimetic lines. Emphasizing that the feeling expressed by a work of art is not the artist's but the intersubjective meaning of a symbolic form, Mrs. Langer insists that "the art-lover who views, hears, or reads a work enters into a direct relation not with the artist, but with the work; he responds to it as he would to a 'natural' symbol." Yet Mrs. Langer also points out that a work of art is more than an arrangement of given things. "Something emerges from the arrangement of tones and colors which was not there before, and this, rather than the arranged material, is the symbol of sentience." In literature, an "illusion of life" results from the arrangement of words; and this illusion, although created by the poet's use of discourse, functions as a "nondiscursive symbolic form" whose artistic import, unlike verbal meaning with its separable units, is "purely implicit in the poem as a totality" (pp. 40, 221, 394). Clearly, Mrs. Langer's concept of the "illusion of life" which at once inheres in, emerges from, and transcends verbal discourse makes her consider literary works from the point of view of the imaginative world they evoke.

Mrs. Langer's observations concerning genre focus on the different kinds of "experiential illusion" brought about by narrative, lyric, and dramatic works. In her clearly articulated opinion, the evocation of virtual life through language involves narration as the structural basis for most works of literature. This "organizing device" suggests the "semblance of memory" because stories told seem to be remembered either by a distinct narrator or some objectified, depersonalized mind. The familiar convention of adapting the presentation of a story to one character's impressions and evaluations merely accentuates the general tendency of narrative to simplify and compose perceptions, as memory does, into units of knowledge. Mrs. Langer concludes that "literature in the strict sense" (that is: narrative literature) creates the illusion of remembered life (pp. 261ff, 293).

In contrast to the "mnemonic projection" of narrative, lyric poems with their frequent use of present tense and direct address do not evoke their world in the mode of virtual past. Mrs. Langer considers an "impersonal subjectivity" as the "peculiar experiential illusion of a genre that creates no characters and no public events." It is not quite clear why the voice of a speaker, this "peculiar experiential illusion" of lyric poems, should be termed "impersonal" (I suspect that

Mrs. Langer wishes thereby to preclude any uncritical identification of the lyric "I" with the poet's biographically amen-
able ego), but the characterization of lyric poetry with
respect to the absence from its world of certain narrative and
dramatic features points to an important aspect of lyric poems
—their relation to thematic modes of discourse (pp. 259f).

The virtual life created by drama is at even further remove
from the mnemonic projection of "literature in the strict
sense." Indeed, Mrs. Langer refuses to regard drama as a
genre of literature proper and revives the Aristotelian concept
of *poesis* to include arts, such as drama and film, whose
"semblance of history" does not rely on language alone. At
the same time, however, she carefully distinguishes drama
(where the words uttered by the characters mark the "cul-
minating points" of action) from its ritualistic origins: "the
minute the two antagonists stepped out of the choric ensemble
and addressed not the deity, nor the congregation, but each
other, they created a poetic illusion and drama was born."
Mrs. Langer describes the generic illusion produced by drama
as a virtual history which, dealing essentially with commit-
ments and consequences, points beyond the present. In contrast to the virtual past of the narrative "Mode of Memory,"
drama's "Mode of Destiny" frames a world of "virtual future." Thus reviving Jean Paul Richter's association of dramatic action with the future, Mrs. Langer suggests that the
demonstration of "what is coming to the doer" is the obvious
subject matter for an art oriented toward consequences;
this is why the "tragic theme" (guilt leading to expiation)
and the "comic theme" (vanity leading to exposure) provide
the most natural means of dramatic construction (pp. 266,
306f, 315, 322, 327). Yet Mrs. Langer also points out that
those familiar "themes" do not reveal the essence of drama.

Nor does she accept them as indispensable determinants of tragedy and comedy: the two "great dramatic forms" ultimately stem from two fundamental "rhythms" of life and thus contrast the human awareness of individuation and death to the immortality, as it were, of species as such and the Protozoa. While comedy exhibits the vital rhythm of nature's self-preservation, tragedy abstracts the rhythm of self-consummation from the irreversible phases of multicellular life: growth, maturity, and decline. Neither genre is, of course, restricted to treat its underlying analogue in a literal sense; tragedy, for instance, tends to imprint the rhythm of "deathward advance" as a perceptible form on matter involving a time span of days or hours instead of the "decades of biological consummation" (pp. 327, 350f, 360f).

Mrs. Langer's practical criticism of comic and tragic works is less impressive than her coherent theoretical approach to problems of genre. Her suggestion that Corneille's and Racine's plays are "heroic comedies" rather than tragedies is particularly overingenious (p. 337). Yet she steers clear of the bias often found in critics who approach the two genres with a preconceived model of the world and expect all writers to have "imitated" their paradigm. Relying on her concept of the "emotive content" of art works as something "prerational and vital, something of the life rhythms we share with all growing, hungering, moving and fearing creatures" (*Philosophy in a New Key*, p. 211), Mrs. Langer does not have to interpret the tragic view of life as an "interim reading" of an ultimately untragic universe. (Cf. Ellis-Fermor, p. 147.) Nor need she, on the other hand, demand that comedy draw a "magic circle" beyond which its reader must not step lest "the wider and deeper view" of the essentially tragic human existence destroy the pattern of the comic world. (Cf. Daiches, p. 238.) Transcending such fallacies of the mimetic approach, Mrs. Langer's comprehensive view of death-bound individual existence within the uninterrupted flow of self-perpetuating life welcomes the poetic presentation of either "rhythm" to the measure of a given work's intrinsic excellence.

As a reviewer of stage productions and the adapter of Pirandello and Brecht to the American stage, Eric Bentley is the most "practical" drama critic surveyed here. Yet his concepts of genre, indebted to such thinkers as Plato and Aristotle, Schopenhauer and Nietzsche, Bergson and Freud, show ample proof of "theoretical" penetration also. Clearly, Bentley's view of drama as the imitation of men's conscious and subconscious conflicts relies on a broader empirical foundation than the actor's stage. It is not surprising, therefore, that in *The Life of the Drama* (1964) Bentley exemplifies his concepts of melodrama, farce, tragedy, comedy, and tragicomedy with frequent references to novels, operas, and motion pictures as well as actual plays.

Melodrama and farce are coupled as the "lower forms" not because they exaggerate—in fact Bentley argues that they do not—but because they are "uninhibited." Melodrama derives its basic formula, innocence surrounded by malevolence, from "more or less paranoid fantasies," and farce exhibits the fierce pleasure of aggression with which "innocence" retaliates. Employing the unrestrained "naturalism of the dream life," both genres appear "childish, savage, sick" from an "adult, civilized, healthy" perspective. Yet their fairy-tale-like features—indulgence in physical violence, naive juxtaposition of perfect heroes and contemptible villains—reflect a certain kind of reality, namely, the reality of subconscious drives. According to Bentley, works belonging to these "lower forms" tend to have a wholesome "cathartic" effect as they help release suppressed fears and desires through the harmless channel of esthetic responses (pp. 203ff, 216f, 223, 246, 255ff).

Tragedy and comedy incorporate important aspects of melodrama and farce, respectively. They are "higher forms" precisely because they transcend rather than exclude the "lower forms." Surely, the heroes and villains of tragedy and the fools and knaves of comedy are more complex than the corresponding character types in melodrama and farce. Yet Bentley insists that the fundamental difference does not lie in differing degrees of verisimilitude: as a villain of tragedy, Iago is by no means "more natural and banal" than Richard III, a melodramatic villain. What really prevents *Othello* from being a melodrama is Shakespeare's subtle division of responsibility. "Iago instigates; Othello is susceptible. Between them, Iago and Othello combine vices of civilization with those of barbarism." Tragedy transcends melodrama as justice transcends revenge: in melodrama, the innocent hero may require suffering; in tragedy, the guilty hero must endure it (pp. 257, 267f, 288f).

Tragedy thwarts our impulse to identify with innocence and exacts identification with guilt, thereby promoting self-knowledge instead of melodrama's wishful gratification of the ego. Comedy promotes self-knowledge in a different fashion. It makes us identify with the author whose wise and detached view of the characters we share. Yet comedy faces the misery of the human condition before it settles down on "the other side of despair." Unlike farce, comedy decides "to look the other way" only after it has seen and taken note. So much can be readily admitted even though Bentley overshoots the mark when he interprets comedy's "Let's not go into that" as "That won't bear going into"—an attitude of "pessimism blacker than tragedy, for tragedy presupposes that everything can be gone into" (pp. 260ff, 298f).

Within the realm of comedy Bentley distinguishes the Latin tradition of "tendentious" and cruel, almost farcical wit from a comforting, rather benevolent vein of humor which includes wit but can also go beyond it. "All comedy before the Elizabethans and most French comedy afterwards" exemplify the former type; Shakespeare, Cervantes, Sterne, Jean Paul Richter, Dickens, Chaplin, Manzoni, Pirandello, Gogol, Chekhov, and Sholem Aleichem are Bentley's signposts for the latter. The details of Bentley's argument are more stimulating than his rather sweeping classification might suggest. Above all, he is clearly right in insisting that there is a price to pay for the "romantic" atmosphere of love and happiness often evoked by the latter type of comedy. It is seldom considered that such an atmosphere can be regarded either as "reality itself or the veil of illusion—as you will." When Mozart turns Beaumarchais's "worldly, witty, Gallic" *Marriage of Figaro* with its obviously ironic happy ending into the "spiritual and humorous" comedy of his opera, he demonstrates (as Shakespeare does in *Twelfth Night* and other romances) that "love and happiness have their reality in art, while the question of their reality in life is left in uncynical abeyance" (pp. 311ff).

In Bentley's opinion, tragedy as well as comedy provide "horribly conclusive evidence that life is not worth living," yet both genres ultimately affirm the value of human existence "in defiance of the stated facts." As the concluding chapter of *The Life of the Drama* implies, this paradox is mitigated in one kind of tragicomedy, emphasized in another. Reviewing traditional concepts of tragicomedy, Bentley discards the pastoral plays of the Renaissance as well as the eighteenth-century "middle genre"—those tearful comedies and bourgeois tragedies in which "comedy lost its breadth and tragedy its depth." His own concept of tragicomedy includes two less limited types of drama: works in which genuine tragedy is encountered and transcended rather than simply averted, and works in which the penetrating eye of comedy refuses "to look the other way." Of the two types the former is, of course, not quite "up to date." It is in essence "tragedy with a comic sequel" elaborating on the final moment of reconciliation—brief if at all present in genuine tragedy. Shakespeare's *Measure for Measure*, Kleist's *Prinz von Homburg*, Goethe's *Iphigenie* and *Faust* are tragicomedies in this sense of the word; they celebrate forgiveness as opposed to "justice," that higher form of revenge. The fact that supreme achievement is so rare in this genre may be due, as Bentley intimates, to the triple standard of our civilization "preaching forgiveness, while believing in justice, while practicing revenge" (pp. 308f, 316ff, 319, 331).

The other, more somber kind of tragicomedy could be described as "comedy with a tragic sequel" except that the mood of the unhappy ending casts its shadow on the entire works belonging to this genre. Ibsen's *Wild Duck*, Chekhov's *Cherry Orchard*, Shaw's *Saint Joan*, Pirandello's *Six Characters*, and Brecht's *Mahagonny* are among Bentley's relatively early examples; and those plays have in a sense prepared the way for such more pronounced expressions of tragicomic despair as Beckett's *Godot* and Ionesco's *Chairs*, to mention only two representatives of the theater of the absurd. While admitting that comic effects intensify rather than lighten the gloom permeating this type of modern drama, Bentley insists that "even gallows humor is humor"; a man who truly lost hope "would not be on hand to say so"—especially not in the form of a work of art. "All art is a challenge to despair," and the seemingly hopeless tragicomedies of the absurd show exceptional courage in addressing themselves to the "peculiarly harrowing, withering despairs of our epoch" (pp. 319f, 334f, 345, 350, 352f).

Bentley spells—and largely interprets—"*tragi-comedy*" with the traditional hyphen. In contrast, Karl S. Guthke's *Modern Tragicomedy* (1966) may be characterized as a study of the circumstances in which the hyphen should be omitted. Guthke recalls that G. E. Lessing, in Section 70 of his *Hamburgische Dramaturgie* (1767–1769), admitted the existence of events in which "gravity provokes laughter, sadness pleasure, or vice versa, so directly that an abstraction of the one or the other is impossible for us"; in portraying such events, Lessing remarked, "art knows how to draw profit from this impossibility." The context of this pronouncement permits Guthke to celebrate Lessing as the first influential champion of the idea that tragic and comic emotions need not be aroused successively in the audience of tragicomedy; they can become, in Guthke's words, "fused inextricably." Applying this "synthetic" rather than additive concept of tragicomedy to Lessing's *Minna von Barnhelm* (1767) and many other plays of considerably later date, Guthke outlines the nature and historical development of a genre largely coextensive with Bentley's second type of "tragi-comedy." It hardly matters that Guthke proposes a troublesome distinction between the "nonsensical world" of the "grotesque-absurd" and the world of genuine tragicomedy—a world which is only "out of joint, with the parts still intact." Discussing Beckett, Ionesco, and Dürrenmatt, Guthke himself ignores that distinction, and rightly so, for it blurs rather than clarifies his central thesis

according to which "the tragicomic is a synthetic phenomenon" in which "the tragic and the comic are identical and
mutual conditions of each other" (pp. IX, 41f, 75).

To be sure, it may be possible and useful to distinguish
predominantly tragic and predominantly comic aspects in
most tragicomedies. Yet Guthke's concept of "synthetic"
tragicomedy directs needed attention to the important difference between works which contrast and works which integrate their tragic and comic implications. Furthermore, the
concept of tragicomedy as "a complex and yet simple genre"
may help to elucidate a great number of modern plays whose
general import, with respect to the tragic-comic dichotomy,
tends to be ironic and ambiguous enough to turn each "seeming statement into an actual question" (pp. 59, 170).

Chapter Four

The Critic and His Horizon

Having surveyed the major themes in twentieth-century genre criticism, we are ready for a more detailed discussion of Georg Lukács's historical and Northrop Frye's archetypal approach to literary classification. I hardly need to say that I admire many insights of both critics. My high opinion of their achievement is the very reason why I will so frequently dwell on what I regard as shortcomings in their respective theories. In order to become aware of the complete horizon against which twentieth-century criticism operates, one should be especially rigorous in dealing with generic concepts that have, or with certain modifications might have, determined our potential range of vision.

1. *Georg Lukács*

Despite the sizable contribution Georg Lukács was making to Marxist theory and Communist practice for over half a century, his literary criticism preserved until his death in 1971 many marks of its initial alignment with the esthetics of German idealism. His various pronouncements on genre at once demonstrate the impressive range and the basic unity of Lukács's critical interests. On his intellectual pilgrimage from neo-Kantian beginnings through Hegel (1914), Marx (1918), and Lenin (1923) to his final attempts at integrating Aristotle's and Goethe's concepts of art with the doctrine of historical materialism, Lukács remained faithful to the view that a small number of genres, each determined by a set of recognizable laws of its own, constitute the realm of literature.

The dialogue form of the long essay on Laurence Sterne ("Reichtum, Chaos und Form," 1909) articulates the critical personality of the early Lukács in a most revealing manner. Whereas Vincenz presents the arguments of the romanticist *manqué* inside the critic's mind, the ardent neoclassicist Joachim seems to be Lukács's more intimate spokesman. In Vincenz's "expressive" opinion, artistic form results from the "enhancement of a powerful sentiment to independent significance." All forms expressing strong feelings strike us indirectly as expressions of our own emotional power and of the infinite richness of the world, but works like Sterne's novels have the same effect in a more immediate fashion: instead of being well-rounded, they are "direct symbols of the infinite" (pp. 268ff). Joachim protests; to his mind, veritable richness depends on the ability to evaluate, and only the power to select is genuine power. His plea for the importance of a fixed point of view relies on the characteristically "mimetic" demand *ut pictura poesis:* "In life one can, nay should, permanently change one's angle of vision in relation to the things one looks at; a work of painting, however, will sovereignly prescribe the direction from which it has to be viewed. It is the consequence of [the artist's] impotence rather than of [his] sovereignty if you must view this part of the picture from one direction and that part of it from another" (p. 294).

The expressive and mimetic positions appear interrelated in the epistolary introduction to *Die Seele und die Formen* (1911). Here Lukács imputes a distinct "psychic content" to every "form" of literature as a correlative of the "moment of destiny" which, like the unification of the hero and his fate defines tragedy, characterizes the "world" typical of a given genre (pp. 16ff). Five years later, however, Lukács propounds an unequivocally "mimetic" *Theorie des Romans* (1916).[1] Under the decisive influence of Hegel's *Esthetics*, Lukács now stresses the connection between the emergence, transformation, and disappearance of genres and the progress of world history. Slighting the importance of the "formative intentions" of particular writers, Lukács's *Theorie de Romans* considers the great epic poem and the novel as necessary literary reflections of successive stages in the historical self-realization of the *Weltgeist* (p. 53).

Although the Marxist Lukács was to recant both the method and the conclusions of his early theory of the novel, the conviction that genre history reflects decisive changes in the history of mankind remained a fundamental premise of his thinking about literature. To be sure, his book *Der historische Roman* (1937)[2] no longer relates human history to such cosmic workings of the world spirit as the elopement of the intrinsic meaning of life from post-Hellenic cultures. Yet the warp in Lukács's first Marxist theories of genre and the one-sided orientation of his Hegelian phase are but different aspects of the same, almost complete, inattention to nuances of literary structure, to the writers' "formative intentions," and to the convention-trained expectations of the reading public. Only his last theoretical work on esthetics, *Die Eigenart des Ästhetischen* (1963), addresses itself explicitly to the

[1] This is the date of the first publication of the long essay in *Zeitschrift für Ästhetik und allgemeine Kunstwissenschaft*. It was first published as a book in 1920.

[2] This is the date of the Russian translation. The German original was first published in 1955.

question of how it is possible to write original masterpieces within the framework of a clearly recognizable generic tradition (I, 660f).

The central concern of Lukács's *Esthetics* can be described as an attempt to combine the concept of artistic *mimesis* as humanized refraction (rather than scientifically accurate reflection) of reality with the tenet that man's problems and values spring from concrete social conflicts of history. Although Lukács relegates the detailed treatment of generic questions to parts of his *Esthetics* which, as we now know, will not be forthcoming, the two volumes already published in 1963 develop and unify many of his previously stated ideas on the subject. First and foremost, Lukács now clarifies his earlier concepts of lyric, narrative, and dramatic literature by expressly describing the three genres as "homogeneous media" whose respective "atmosphere" allows an infinite number, yet strictly defined kind, of subject matters to become integrated into works that belong to the given genre (I, 640ff). It is also important that Lukács's *Esthetics* states as a general rule that the "laws" of a genre can only be observed through a writer's creatively up-to-date extension of their scope (I, 660). This principle qualifies the "objective" function Lukács assigns to the literary artist's subjectivity—the function, as it were, of a wondrous prism that selects and intensifies those "rays" emanating from a given moment of human history which are particularly significant for the present and the future of mankind (II, 838ff *et passim*).

It is possible that his cooperation with the short-lived *Thalia*—a Budapest art theater founded in 1904 by oppositional intellectuals—imposed on young Lukács a sense of the limitations of the modern stage. In the long Introduction

(1909) to his Hungarian *History of the Development of Modern Drama* (1911) Lukács deplores the rationalistic rather than mythic origin of bourgeois drama: its substitution of excessive interest in psychopathology for the mythological focus on fate. Lukács argues that the inner conflicts of insulated characters cannot constitute genuine dialogue—the simultaneous use of word as symbolic *and* natural utterances (pp. 305, 678f, 690). Preferring the Greek tragedians' "simple monumentality" to Shakespeare's "variegated diversity," the early Lukács hoped for a rejoinder to Lessing's *Hamburgische Dramaturgie* (1767–1969) and perhaps intended to write "the new dramaturgy: for Corneille and against Shakespeare" himself (*Die Seele und die Formen*, pp. 6, 351, 367f). But he was also willing to commend less time-honored artistic intentions than those of Periclean tragedy, provided that they did not claim rights to an esthetic medium originally developed in connection with another genre. In his astonishingly early "Gedanken zu einer Ästhetik des Kinos" (1913) Lukács hailed the art of the cinema as an instrument which would prove just as adequate for the "scenic yearning" of an Achim von Arnim or Edgar Allan Poe of the day as the Greek stage was for Sophocles (p. 79). It seems, therefore, that theoretical purism rather than esthetic insensitivity induced Lukács to devise, in his *Theorie des Romans*, a scheme of literature in which dramatic perfection was exclusively associated with ancient Greece, and the greatest post-Hellenic playwright (despite his readily acknowledged "exuberant fullness") could merely serve to illustrate the unwholesome "polarization" of more recent tragedy around the stylistic antipodes Shakespeare and Alfieri (pp. 36, 50). In short, there is no use denying that the genre theoretician and the art lover in Lukács were to find their common ground for the appreciation of Renaissance and later drama under the influence of that great admirer of Shakespeare—Karl Marx.

In *Der historische Roman*, Lukács adapts Hegel's concept of the Greek tragic heroes as the embodiments of conflicting "goals" (*Zwecke*) of world history to the Marxist view of history as the history of class struggles. But whereas Hegel and the early Lukács contrasted Greek tragedy as the symbolic representation of the substance of a historical collision to later tragic drama relying on the subjective inner conflicts of the characters, the Marxist Lukács argues that every great tragedy ultimately springs from an objective social conflict (p. 124). Shakespeare's historical plays, for instance, reflect "the welter of contradiction which filled the uneven but fatal path of feudal crisis over centuries" without simplifying the process down to a mechanical contrast between the "old" and the "new." "Shakespeare sees the triumphant humanist character of the rising new world but also sees it causing the breakdown of a patriarchal society humanly and morally better in many respects and more closely bound to the interest of the people" (p. 185). Although this statement could be regarded as a Marxist's convincing explanation why Shakespeare cannot be very profitably analyzed in Marxian terms, it also supports Lukács's verdict concerning the generic issue involved: Shakespeare's drama had to reflect a more complex state of affairs than Periclean tragedy, and "precisely because the quintessence of drama relies on the same principles with Shakespeare and with the Greeks, the dramatic form of his plays was to become completely different" (p. 114). Clearly, the Marxist view that the central problems of mankind are historically determined motivates Lukács's newly acquired appreciation of the non-Hellenic breadth in Shakespeare's plays.

The Hegelian Lukács could demand in a metaphysical

sense that drama manifest the "intensive totality of substance." The Marxist Lukács regards substance as the universal aspect of empirical reality: the "historically necessary" transformation of social order through a seemingly haphazard sequence of events, or the conformity (usually expressed by natural laws) between individual occurrences. Associating drama with the esthetic revelation of this empirical kind of substance, he now argues that the playwright's relative neglect of what leads up to and down from the essential turning points of an action—his almost exclusive interest in the making of important decisions, the calling-to-account of a person, and other "dramatic facts of life"—need not distort, nor transcend, reality. In spite of its seeming remoteness from ordinary life, the concentrated and intensified world of a drama reveals the universal aspects inherent in, but hidden behind the surface of, actual phenomena (pp. 126, 119ff; cf. *Die Theorie des Romans*, p. 41f).

Attempting to keep his universals historically concrete, Lukács warns against deriving a tragic world view from the mood of some of the most overwhelming works of literature. In his opinion, almost every great tragedy reflects the essence of a specific social conflict rather than some eternal predicament of the *conditio humana*. The character of an Antigone, Romeo, or Othello does not by necessity lead to the destruction of those tragic figures; the outcome of the respective plays results, Lukács argues, from "concrete historical collisions" in which those figures find themselves entangled (p. 188). Only in his late essay (1963) on Lessing's *Minna von Barnhelm* does Lukács consider at least one type of inner conflict—the contradiction between the demands of some historically conditioned morality and a more universally human ethical principle—as evoking the full depth of genuine tragedy. This emancipation of drama from the tyranny of concrete history not only refines Lukács's concept of the tragic, but also enables him to assume (for the first time, I believe, in the course of his critical odyssey) a stimulating attitude toward the world of comedy. Lukács contrasts two groups of Lessing's plays: while in *Philotas* (1759) and *Emilia Galotti* (1772) the playwright intimates that an aspect of inhuman brutality may be admixed to the exercise of otherwise commendable virtues, his *Minna von Barnhelm* (1767) and *Nathan der Weise* (1779) succeed in evoking and still overruling the effects of that tragic dichotomy. Nathan's tolerant wisdom overcomes the "danger of responding to external inhumanity in kind" (p. 30), and the same feat is accomplished by Minna's gracefully common-sense desire for relaxed happiness in the framework of society (p. 34). Discussing Lessing's high comedies as dramatic "fairy tales of the Enlightenment" (*Aufklärungsmärchen*, p. 34), Lukács still looks at esthetic phenomena from a historical point of view. But such a reasonably limited residue of the historical perspective seems to me an asset rather than a shortcoming in any approach to literature.

In his *History of the Development of Modern Drama*, Lukács merely distinguished modern life as destroying human beings through the "epic totality" of petty collisions from a more dignified era congenial with the great single blows of tragedy (p. 692). In *Die Theorie des Romans*, however, he expounded his early view of narrative literature more fully. This (implicitly) very systematic book suggests (1) a qualitative distintion between drama and the "large narrative forms" (*große Epik*) as directed, respectively, toward the "intensive totality of the substance" and the "extensive totality of life"; (2) a quantitative distinction between large and small narrative forms as characterized by their respective capacity to encompass life as a whole or merely one section of it; and (3) a historical distinction between the two large narrative forms: whereas Homer could shape his works—"strictly speaking the only genuine epics"—with the harmonious concrete totality of Greek life as their supposed model taken for granted, the modern novelist must search (and make his heroes search) for meaning and harmony in a world that permanently disintegrates into abstract objects and conventions on the one hand and the onlooker's subjectivity on the other. Each of these distinctions reveals one of three closely related aspects in the precarious generic position of the novel. First, the novel is to impart a sense of extensive totality and must not follow drama's intensifying recourse to the substance; yet its actual extent is no more "infinite" than the extent of any palpably selective small narrative form. Next, since the novel is to reflect life as an objectively given totality, its world must not appear as resulting from conscious selection and willful interpretation; yet its narrative structure presupposes the semblance of a narrator's more or less overt subjectivity. Finally, life as a whole can only be reflected by a narrative work if a meaningful interdependence of objective and subjective forces prevails in the writer's world; yet no such pattern of order, Lukács argues, is discernibly inherent in the post-Grecian world (pp. 23f, 44ff, 57f, 76f, 132).

In Lukács's view, then, the fragmentary character of modern life, its rigid separation of subject from object, does not allow for such a felicitous resolution of the "generic dissonance" underlying the large narrative forms as was Homer's reduction of the narrator's subjectivity to a "mute and astonished gaze" (p. 45). But the novelist (largely identified by

Lukács with the narrator of a novel) may "go subjective" to the extreme point at which his subjectivity annihilates itself and thus achieves the "self-correction of fragmentaries" (pp. 73f, 93). Following hints of Friedrich Schlegel and Karl Solger, Lukács discerns a form of irony as the central principle of organization in those narrative masterpieces that have succeeded in turning the threefold generic predicament of the novel into high esthetic values. Such ironic works often lead up to the self-recognition of a problematical individual as necessarily and forever problematical, thereby providing a sudden insight from the ideal perspective of what *should* be, into a reality that should *not* (p. 79).

Lukács's *Theorie des Romans* is clearly not a theory of Fielding's and Jane Austen's, Thackeray's and George Eliot's novels. These and several other supremely gifted writers of prose fiction must remain without mention in the long essay, concentrating on certain characteristics of Cervantes, Goethe, Flaubert, and Tolstoy, for a simple reason: Lukács discusses a definite type of world one kind of novel appears to reflect, and not the great variety of narrative techniques the novel has developed to evoke many different types of worlds. If the ironic "melancholy of having grown up" informs the world of a large narrative form, Lukács is willing to consider it as a genuine novel even though, according to his own argument, a version of lyricism on the part of the characters and a meditative bent on the part of the narrator is likely to characterize such works (pp. 78, 85). But the same marks of unrepressed subjectivity seem to Lukács to preclude the grasp of extensive totality if they occur in works that he chooses to classify as small narrative forms. Neither Charles Louis Philippe's treatment of psychic impulses as an action, nor Heinrich von Kleist's "cool and superior gesture of the chronist" revealing demonic abysses of fate in and through apparent coincidence, can evoke life in its totality because, in *this* connection Lukács insists, both the lyric stress on subjective experience and the lyric element in the careful "selection" from life of a symbolic event counteract the generic principles of the novel (pp. 45ff). Despite the inconsistency involved, Lukács's early awarenes of such phenomena as the complex lyric quality of a dramatized consciousness and the lyric (or in fact rather authorial) aspect of even the most scenic narration might have prompted valuable insights into the manner in which language evokes world, had Lukács been, or had he later become, more interested in the verbal structure of *mimesis*.

Obviously enough, however, Lukács's 1937 reinterpretation of the "large narrative forms" shows no more concern for verbal structure than his Marxist reinterpretation of his earlier concept of tragedy does. In *Der historische Roman* Lukács argues that the process of complication in the social fabric of emerging capitalism found its literary reflection in the emergence of the novel as a distinct genre. In industrial societies, an individual's class status does not determine his intellectual physiognomy to the same extent as rank or estate defined the personality of its members in earlier times; yet the novel can reflect complex social collisions by elaborating on their larger, less dramatic context (pp. 169ff). This holds also for historical novels which must, therefore, beware of placing a great figure of history in their center. Sir Walter Scott is the "father of the historical novel" precisely because the human embodiments of "combating extremes," the conspicuous heroes of history, appear on the periphery of his best works while the vicissitudes of some average Englishman sustain the mainstream of narrative. Lukács does not regard this principle of plot organization as a mere "trick" or clever device. Scott's characteristic plot structure strikes him rather as the "compository expression" of an acute sense of history enabling Sir Walter to avoid two opposed pitfalls: the "romantic monumentalization" as well as the "psychological abasement" of great historical figures. Introducing them only at occasions when these figures fulfill their "historic mission" in a crisis already delineated in the "capillary medium" of everyday life, Scott makes his reader apprehend the objective historical, not the subjective personal, genesis of historic greatness (pp. 43f, 46, 57).

Lukács argues that the emergence of what is known as the historical novel was conditioned by the increased awareness of history permeating Europe after the French Revolution of 1789 and the Napoleonic wars. For the Marxist Lukács, however, every great novel is basically historical because it reflects "the self-reproduction of society, its tendencies of gradual development upwards and downwards" through concrete details of the everyday lives of typical individuals (p. 181). Despite his lip service to the novel's "capillary medium" of *mimesis*, Lukács remains too much of a neoclassicist to endorse a naturalistic interest in outward detail or the microscopic focus of different stream-of-consciousness techniques on a mind. He would discuss "naturalism" and "psychologism" as decadent trends of bourgeois literature, and even blame their advocates for apologetically implying that the alienation of man's natural and social environment from his subjectivity is part and parcel of the human condition rather than a temporary evil of capitalism. (Cf. "Erzählen oder Beschreiben?", 1936, and *Wider den mißverstandenen Realismus*, 1957.) I cannot help suspecting that under the new ideological superstructure Joachim's conservative taste—fa-

miliar to us from the early dialogue on Laurence Sterne—
motivates Lukács's rejection of Zola, Proust, Joyce, and their
disciples.

Lukács follows Hegel in contrasting the great epic poem as
a representation of a "total world" to drama as a much more
selective genre characterized by "total movement." Having
allied the novel with the great epic poem as the second "large
narrative form," he faces the task of discovering significant
similarities and differences between the sharp but relatively
small mimetic focus of drama and the generic scope of shorter
narratives. In *Die Theorie des Romans*, Lukács distinguished
three "small narrative forms": *Novelle, Idylle, "Chantefable."*
Only the first named remained in the center of his later critical interest. Like many other critics in the German tradition,
Lukács separates the *Novelle* as a highly artistic form from
the ordinary short story (*Erzählung*) of much lower standing;
by merely designating a narrative work as a *Novelle*, Lukács
implies positive value judgments concerning its high degree
of coherence, almost "dramatic" sweep, and far-reaching
symbolic import. According to Lukács's Marxist concept of
the *Novelle*, its selection of an extraordinary and seemingly
accidental occurrence from the totality of life does not result
from a writer's arbitrary choice but reflects in a nutshell the
totality of a certain kind of life whose framework is capable
of containing such an "extreme case" (Cf. "Gottfried Keller,"
1939, pp. 375ff, and "Solschenizyn: Ein Tag im Leben des
Iwan Denissowitsch," 1964, pp. 545f). As it stands, this tenet
is surely overingenious. Yet the great evocative power of
many *Novellen* might well result from their authors' careful
choice of unusual yet symbolically meaningful incidents occurring in extreme human situations. For example, Lukács and
his fellow-revisionist friend, the Austrian critic Ernst Fischer,

doubtless knew what they were talking about when they discussed, very broad-mindedly indeed, Solzhenitsyn's account of one day in a Siberian concentration camp as a penetrating symbol of everyday life in Stalin's larger "Socialist Camp."

The Marxist Lukács's remarks on the lyric genre modify and clarify rather than contradict his earlier view of the same subject. To be sure, that view was first formulated in a rather cryptic manner. In *Die Seele und die Formen* Lukács insisted that the "unification of the soul and the background" constitutes the lyric "moment of destiny" (p. 18), and in *Die Theorie des Romans* he described what the lyric evokes as "a Protean mythology of the substantial subjectivity" (p. 60). Yet some of Lukács's early views on lyric poetry were to re-emerge as a rather articulate "mimetic" interpretation of this "expressive" genre.

According to a grandiose suggestion of *Die Theorie des Romans*, Nature and the Soul appear meaningfully united or, at least, *meaningfully* separated in those great "lyric moments" in which Nature, even in our sense-forsaken post-Grecian world, reveals itself as a legible symbol while the Soul "coagulates" to the point of assuming the physical state, as it were, of the substance (p. 61). Pointing out about fifty years later that the poet selects those aspects of the exterior world which promote the evocation of a certain mood through their symbolic power, Lukács propounds a more sober view of the correspondence, intimated by nature poetry, between "subjective" moods and "objective" phenomena. And the Marxist Lukács does not slight the importance of such "objective" means for the expression of something "subjective"; rather, he quotes six lines from T. S. Eliot's "The Hollow Men" to prove that even the "innermost" can only be given artistic shape by the roundabout way of "reflecting" (that is: using images suggested by) "outward reality" (*Ästhetik*, I, 662f, II, 638). Thus Lukács has abandoned the premature metaphysics inherent in his earlier approach to the lyric without losing sight of an important characteristic of lyric poetry: its great capacity of interrelating inner and outer "worlds."

Lukács remained faithful to the more solid part of another one of his early tenets also. In *Die Theorie des Romans*, he discussed the functions of time in different genres and concluded that the lyric poet neither places objects in the monumental "timelessness" of drama or the great epic poem, nor does he submerge them in an "atmosphere of elapsing time" characteristic of novels; the poet's realm is the process of remembrance or oblivion, and in this process objects merely serve as the occasion for experience (p. 131). His peculiar terminology notwithstanding, the Marxist Lukács holds a similar but more reasonable view when he remarks that lyric poetry reflects, in addition to reality, the very act by which the writer's mind "reflects" reality. In his last period, Lukács even disentangles the lyric "process of reflection" from the ordinary emotions of a particular human being. His suggestion that Keats has captured a "typical" succession of feeling in his "Ode to a Nightingale" commends itself by its uncompromising refusal to associate the emotive content of the poem with any single emotional experience in the mind, or the soul, of the poet (*Ästhetik*, I, 663; II, 668f).

In his *Esthetics*, Lukács offers an interesting solution to the problem of how some great works of polemical or didactic literature could retain their artistic effectiveness even though most of their teaching had long been superseded by new insights in the history of thought. He recapitulates Ivan Petrovich Pavlov's distinction between natural signs (such as

the smell of food acting on "unconditioned reflexes") and artificial signs (such as the sound of a bell, repeatedly rung before feeding, to which a dog's salivary gland will soon start to
respond with a "conditioned reflex"). Lukács postulates the
existence of a third "system of signals" which, on the human
level of consciousness, combines the abstract, "scientific"
dimension of artificial signs with the concreteness of natural
ones; he argues that the arts, each in a way that is adequate
to its particular medium, invite highly complex responses
to this third kind of signs or signals (II, 99ff). The poetic
use of language, for instance, appeals to a mode of perception
which can sense the "pathos of experienced truth" and the
"poetic form of conceptual rightness" in such works as *De
rerum natura* or *Divina commedia*, even though the ever-ad-
vancing scientific reflection of reality has disproved most
tenets propounded by Lucretius and Dante (II, 167f). But
Lukács also insists that the ideas expressed in literature must
not be ideas of an "abstract subject." In meditative poetry
(*Gedankenlyrik*) the writer's conceptual generalizations will
only remain within the esthetic dimensions of literary art if
he succeeds in transforming his subjectivity into a "concrete
figure" (that is, I suppose, into a palpably characterized
speaker in his poem) who can function as the "historical
subject" of a concrete conceptual experience (II, 184).

There can be no doubt that certain essays—Montaigne's
and Oscar Wilde's come readily to mind—meet the same
generic requirement: they establish verbal contact and a high
degree of empathy between a vividly implied author and the
reader whether or not the latter shares the opinions of the
former. Indeed, the Introduction to *Die Seele und die Formen*
characterized the essay as an almost fully qualified literary
genre emerging from the emotive experience of conceptual

thinking. Informed by the writer's incessant search for a system of values, the generic form of the essay relies, Lukács argued in 1911, on the process of evaluation rather than on the verdicts eventually passed (pp. 15ff, 38). Strictly distinguishing the esthetic "reflection" of reality from the conceptual, the Marxist Lukács was to exclude the essay from the realm of imaginative literature. It seems to me, however, that his 1963 concept of the lyric as the reflection not only of reality but also of the process by which a mind reflects reality, leaves the door of verbal art wide open for such genres as the impassioned oratory, the elegantly streamlined proverb or aphorism, and the artistic essay.

As the foregoing pages were intended to demonstrate, Lukács's massive critical work can contribute a good deal to the study of literary genres. My own indebtedness to Lukács will become more obvious when in the next chapter I will suggest a way of divorcing his concepts of the lyric "moment," dramatic "movement," and epic "totality" from their troublesome speculative contexts. Yet, some of Lukács's overgeneralized statements clearly defy any attempt at verification or falsification by the analysis of literary works; as a result, they hardly promote the advance of knowledge in the area of literary criticism. This holds for Lukács's blanket revival of the Hegelian view that every genre emerges and flourishes when its principle of mimetic stylization coincides with the given phase in the historical development of mankind. Even more objectionable is another one of Lukács's basic tenets postulating that the "homogeneous medium" of one, and only one, genre determines the choice and treatment of subject matter in every great work of literature. Indeed, a light stroke of irony, often administered by the arts to their excessively self-reliant theoreticians, appears in the circumstance that the purist Lukács could not help but discuss Goethe's *Faust* and Pushkin's *Onegin* (two works for which he finds only words of the highest praise) as combining in their mode of *mimesis* structural aspects of the lyric, epic, and dramatic genres. (Cf. "Faust-Studien," 1940, pp. 601ff and "Puschkins Platz in der Weltliteratur," 1949, p. 45.)

2. *Northrop Frye*

In the Fourth Essay of Northrop Frye's *Anatomy of Criticism* (1957) we read: "The purpose of criticism by genres is not so much to classify as to clarify traditions and affinities, thereby bringing out a large number of literary relationships that would not be noticed as long as there were no context established for them" (pp. 247f). On such a view, the greater part of Frye's critical work can be interpreted as a most ambitious theory of genre. To be sure, the very term "genre" is used in at least two rather different senses throughout the *Anatomy* and Frye's less important writings: sometimes it applies to specific conventions of plot structure, at other times to general features of verbal structure. Furthermore, while the full title of the Fourth Essay announces a discourse on "Rhetorical Criticism: Theory of Genres," the Second Essay of the *Anatomy* bluntly declares that "nothing is more striking in rhetorical criticism than the absence of any consideration of genre" (p. 95). A more cautious critic would no doubt have avoided this terminological confusion; yet the breadth and depth of insights more than compensate for the occasional imprecision of terms and concepts in Frye's critical system.

While challenging the view that "*a* poem is *an* imitation of nature," Frye suggests that literature considered as an "order of words" imitates "the order of nature as a whole"

(p. 96). Of course, Frye distinguishes nature as the content of art from nature conceived as the environment or occasion of art. As the environment of art, nature and especially human life provide "the seed-plot of literature: a vast mass of potential literary forms, only a few of which will grow up into the greater literary universe" (p. 122). Nature as the content of art is in turn a realm of almost unlimited possibilities. Stretching "from the complete fulfillment of human desire to what human desire utterly repudiates," it follows the patterns not of the actual world but of human imagination (*The Well-Tempered Critic*, 1963, pp. 121f, 155).

The Third Essay of Frye's *Anatomy of Criticism* is devoted to the classification of those imaginative patterns. Frye postulates the existence of four "narrative categories of literature broader than, or logically prior to literary genres" (p. 162). In the course of impressively large-scale speculations concerning plot structure, he attempts to place every story that can be told on a gigantic conceptual map with the "romantic," the "tragic," the "comic," and the "ironic" (or "satiric") as points of compass. The four "generic plots" or *mythoi* emerge as movements within a highly desirable world (romance), within a painfully defective world (irony and satire), downward from innocence through hamartia to catastrophe (tragedy), or upward from the world of experience through threatening complications to "a general assumption of post-dated innocence in which everyone lives happily ever after" (comedy) (p. 162). Dividing each of his four *mythoi* into six phases, Frye, arrives at a "somewhat forbidding piece of symmetry" (p. 177): three phases of both tragedy and comedy parallel phases of irony/satire while the other three correspond to phases of romance. Rather than recapitulate Frye's lengthy discussion of the twenty-four "phases," I am inserting a chart which, I hope, succeeds in tracing Frye's conceptual blueprint.

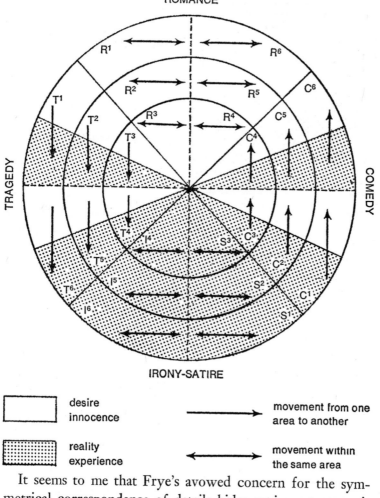

It seems to me that Frye's avowed concern for the symmetrical correspondence of details hides an important merit of his "theory of myths." A second, much simpler diagram may serve to clarify the fact that Frye's theory distinguishes works which evoke a homogeneous world from works whose world is capable of changing radically.

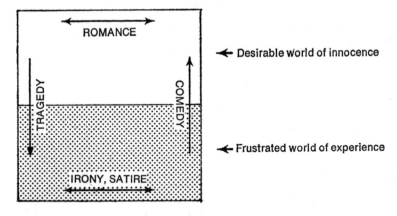

Frye's treatment of the radically changing worlds of tragedy and comedy connects aspects of difference with aspects of similarity in a most stimulating manner. Commenting on God's words about man in *Paradise Lost*—"Sufficient to have stood, though free to fall"—Frye points out that Adam loses freedom by his very use of freedom "just as, for a man who deliberately jumps off a precipice, the law of gravitation acts as fate for the brief remainder of his life." In Frye's view of tragedy, the same act of "narrowing a comparatively free life into a process of causation" is performed by Macbeth when he accepts the logic of usurpation, by Hamlet when he accepts the logic of revenge, and by Lear when he accepts the logic of abdication (pp. 211f). The plot structure of comedy reverses the process and leads the hero out of bondage into a "stable and harmonious order" which, at the end of most comic works, reveals itself to have been only temporarily "disrupted by folly, obsession, forgetfulness, 'pride and prejudice'" (p. 171). Whereas a congenially happy society forms around the hero of comedy, the chorus and the so-called chorus characters usually represent the society from which the tragic hero is gradually isolated. Therefore, chorus and chorus characters are "the embryonic germ of comedy in tragedy, just as the refuser of festivity, the melancholy Jaques or Alceste, is a tragic germ in comedy" (p. 218).

Without explicit reference to Ludwig Jekels's psychoanalytical paper, "On the Psychology of Comedy" (first published in German in 1926), Frye discusses the basic pattern of that genre in a strikingly similar manner. "What normally happens is that a young man wants a young woman, that his desire is resisted by some opposition, usually paternal, and that near the end of the play some twist in the plot enables the hero to have his will" (p. 163). Having said so much, Frye has prepared his reader to consider as characteristic of comedy "a kind of comic Oedipus situation in which the hero replaces his father as a lover." In extreme yet revealing instances, even "fear of violating a mother" occurs in otherwise comic works such as *The Marriage of Figaro* and *Tom Jones*. More frequently, however, no more than "psychological alliance" is expressed or implied between the hero's bride and his or her (step-)mother (pp. 180f). On the paternal side, the hero's way to happiness is often obstructed by his own father who may or may not be his rival for the heroine's love. But the difficulties can also arise in connection with such "father surrogates" as the girl's father, her guardian, or a suitor who is older and wealthier than the hero and thus "partakes of the father's closer relation to established society." With this sociological hint Frye supersedes Jekels, who simply argued that comedy lifts our spirits by displacing Oedipal guilt and the concomitant punishment from son to father. Frye in turn notes how frequently comic works add social criticism to their attack on those who claim—usurp—paternal authority over the young lovers; "some sharp observation of the rising power of money and the sort of ruling class it is building up" can be found as early as in Renaissance playwrights, including Ben Jonson (pp. 163ff).

On the whole, of course, Frye's view of comedy as one of the four *mythoi* is far less indebted to Freud, Marx, and their respective followers than it is to Sir James Frazer's and Carl Gustav Jung's writings on mythology. In the *Anatomy* and elsewhere Frye makes it abundantly clear that he regards the four generic plots as four phases in mankind's most comprehensive myths suggested by the "natural cycle" around the clock (dawn, zenith, sunset, darkness) and the calendar (spring, summer, fall, winter). But the obvious inconsistency in Frye's interrelation of seasonal myths and literary genres betrays the contingent nature of the analogy between the world of literary works and a mythical archetype. Whereas an earlier paper of Frye's, "The Archetypes of Literature" (1951), associates comedy with the summer phase and romance with the spring phase of the "natural cycle," the third essay in *Anatomy of Criticism* elaborates on the four *mythoi* in the following order: The Mythos of Spring: Comedy; The Mythos of Summer: Romance; The Mythos of Autumn: Tragedy; The Mythos of Winter: Irony and Satire. Far from settling the issue in an unequivocal manner, Frye's recent study of Shakespearean comedy and romance implies yet another version of the supposed correspondence between "the order of nature" and literature; in *A Natural Perspective* (1965) Frye relates tragedy *and* irony to the "movement from birth to death, spring to winter, dawn to dark," and comedy *and* romance to the second half of the cycle "moving from death to rebirth, decadence to renewal, winter to spring, darkness to a new dawn" (pp. 119ff).

Remarking in *Anatomy of Criticism* that "the ritual pattern behind the catharsis of comedy is the resurrection that follows death," Frye in that book insists that the scope of comedy is more inclusive than the scope of tragedy; comedy can contain a fully fledged tragedy whereas tragedy tends to employ a comic action "only episodically as a subordinate contrast" (pp. 215f). I doubt whether Frye's theologically motivated bias for comedy can yield useful principles of practical criticism. There is indeed some indication that Frye may eventually assign equal mythic dignity to comedy and tragedy. In a highly instructive passage of *A Natural Perspective*, he rejects both farce and melodrama as uniform dramatic structures and pleads—without any intimation that comedy might provide a more inclusive framework—for the simultaneous presence of "majority and minority moods" in both tragic and comic drama (pp. 48ff).

As archetypes of plot structure, Comedy, Romance, Tragedy and Irony reveal four basic patterns of the human imagination. In the First Essay of the *Anatomy*, Frye argues that all such patterns manifest themselves most clearly in myths, since gods possess the greatest possible power of action, and stories about them "operate on the top level of human desire." As the opposite extreme of literary design, naturalism "displaces" the motifs of myths—the "structural principles of literature"—into contexts of plausibilty while less radical techniques of displacement produce intermediate degrees of verisimilitude. To articulate his concept of displacement, Frye reconsiders Aristotle's generic distinctions according to the "objects of mimesis" and distinguishes five "modes" of literature with regard to the "power of action" attributed to the main characters. (1) The hero of undisplaced myth is a divine being and thus superior in kind both to men and their natural environment. (2) The typical hero of romance, legend, and *märchen* is superior to other men not in kind but only in degree; still, in the world evoked by this group of works, the ordinary laws of nature are "slightly suspended." (3) Superior in degree to other men but subject to his natural environment is the hero of most epic and tragedy—the leader. (4) Approximately equal to other members of his society, the "hero" of most comedy and realistic fiction appears to be "one of us." To myth, romance, aristocratic "high mimetic" and realistic "low mimetic" Frye adds (5) the mode of irony. Leaving the point of "low mimetic" verisimilitude behind, this *mode*—which is not to be confused with the *mythos* of irony—shows us characters "inferior in power or intelligence to ourselves, so that we have the sense of looking down on a scene of bondage, frustration, or absurdity." With such "ironic" works as Kafka's *Trial*, modern literature recoils, so to speak, from the realm of plausibility to the mode of myth, for "the dim outlines of sacrificial rituals and dying gods begin to reappear in it" (pp. 33f, 42). This reference to the mythic reality of dying gods indicates Frye's implicit awareness of the fact that myths can be projections of human fears as well as human aspirations.

Frye's theory of the historical progress of displacement from myth to the low-mimetic mode parallels Victor Hugo's famous pseudohistorical discussion of genres. In the Preface to his play *Cromwell* (1827) Hugo speaks of a gradual process of maturing in the course of which mankind has successively expressed its essential nature in lyric, epic, and dramatic forms. With the Old Testament, Homer, and Shakespeare as primary examples in mind, Hugo suggests that primitive times are lyric, ancient times epic, modern times dramatic; that the ode sings the praise of eternity, the great epic poem celebrates history, drama paints life; and that the ode derives its vigor from the ideal, the epic poem from the grand, and drama from the real (pp. 422f). On the accompanying chart, the left arrow indicates the direction of displacement as described in Frye's *Anatomy*, and the right arrow represents Hugo's view of the "growing up" or maturing of mankind:

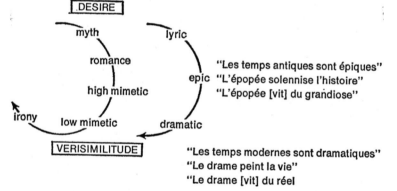

Frye

Hugo

"Les temps primitifs sont lyriques"
"L'ode chante l'éternité"
"L'ode vit de l'idéal"

DESIRE

myth   lyric

romance

"Les temps antiques sont épiques"
epic "L'épopée solennise l'histoire"
high mimetic   "L'épopée [vit] du grandiose"

irony   low mimetic   dramatic

VERISIMILITUDE

"Les temps modernes sont dramatiques"
"Le drame peint la vie"
"Le drame [vit] du réel

I believe that Frye has improved on Hugo in at least two respects. Restricting his concept of "mode" to the world literary works evoke, he does not superimpose distinctions relying on mimetic "spirit"—concern for eternity and the

ideal, history and the grand, or life and the real—on a classification of verbal "form"—lyric, epic, and dramatic structure. Furthermore, Frye specifically allows for "modal
counterpoint" as characteristic of the subtlety of great literature. As an example, he cites Shakespeare's *Antony and
Cleopatra*. The "tonality" of this play showing the fall of a
great leader is high mimetic, but we may also look at Mark
Antony "ironically, as a man enslaved by passion" (pp. 50f).
Despite the possibility of such interplay between different
modes, Frye seems justified in describing a historical tendency to diminish the hero's power of action both in classical antiquity and in the western tradition since the early
Middle Ages.

Frye's historical account of the "themes" of literature as
similarly displaced versions of their archetypes is less convincing. Yet his general remarks on theme—Frye's term for
Aristotle's *dianoia*, usually translated as "thought"—seem to
me highly stimulating indeed. Frye argues that while plot
or *mythos* determines the temporal shape of a work as the
sequence of hypothetical events, theme or *dianoia* holds the
work together in a simultaneous, quasi-spatial pattern of
meaning. The relative prevalence of plot or theme will
make some works primarily "fictional," others primarily
"thematic." Yet *mythos* and *dianoia* emerge as complementary aspects of all literature: "the *mythos* is the *dianoia* in
movement, the *dianoia* is the *mythos* in *stasis*." Frye articulates the difference between the two basic types of literature
in a most suggestive manner: predominantly fictional works
focus on the "internal fiction of the hero and his society";
predominantly thematic works in turn establish a kind of
"external fiction" by emphasizing the contemporaneous or

posthumous relation between the writer and *his* society—
the potential reading public (pp. 52f, 83).

The relative proximity of works to the fictional or the
thematic extreme of literature is one of Frye's concerns in
the Fourth Essay of the *Anatomy*. Here Frye argues that
literary works consist of what ideally are spoken, printed,
chanted, and acted verbal structures (pp. 246f) establishing
different "conditions" between the poet and his public. Works
in which the poet addresses his audience belong to the genre
of *epos* (we are reminded that by *ta epe* the Greeks meant
poems to be recited) while *fiction*, a far less palpably authorial subdivision of literature, appears designed for the
printed page. The "singer" of *lyric* poems pretends to be
communing with himself or, at any rate, with someone other
than his actual listener or reader who, in John Stuart Mill's
phrase, overhears rather than hears the lyric utterances.
Finally and most conventionally, the unmediated presence
of hypothetical figures points to acting as the "radical of
presentation" characteristic of *drama*. Aware of the imaginative status of literature Frye, of course, does not identify
the "radicals" of epos, fiction, lyric, and drama with the
ordinary conduct of language. He considers each of the four
genres as an approximation or *mimesis* of the verbal "rhythm"
underlying direct address, assertive writing, mental association, and conversation, respectively (pp. 246ff).

Although all genres may and, since the invention of the
printing press, increasingly do exist in written form, Frye's
concept of the radical of presentation as the criterion for
generic distinctions appears convincing in the light of his
witty analogy of the keyboard. "Just as it is possible to dis-

tinguish genuine piano music from the piano score of an operetta or symphony, so we may distinguish genuine 'book literature' from books containing the reduced textual scores of recited or acted pieces" (p. 248). Thus, for example, even the least stagelike closet drama of a romantic poet can be seen as being "referred back to some kind of theatre, however much of a castle in the air," and in Joseph Conrad's novels "the genre of the written word is being assimilated to that of the spoken one" through the introduction of internal narrators (p. 247). At their purest, the individual radicals of presentation require that either the poet (drama) or the hypothetical figures (epos) or both the poet and the hypothetical figures (fiction) remain "concealed" from the audience, or else that the audience "be concealed from the poet" (lyric) (p. 249).

I find Frye's fourfold classification of verbal structure illuminating, yet cannot agree with his distinction between "epos" and "fiction" in the realm of narrative literature. The predominantly scenic structure of the most characteristic narrative works written in the "epos" form (according to Frye: the "mimesis of direct address") highlights the towering "hypothetical figures" and conceals their modest chronicler—the traveling rhapsodist. In contrast, "prose fiction" (in Frye's opinion: the mimesis of rather impersonal "assertive writing") had had a long way to go before it became fashionable for nineteenth-century narrators to refrain from overtly intruding into the story and directly addressing the reader. Indeed, Frye himself suggests that the occasional waiver of a given type of "concealment" easily results in various combinations of two or more generic "rhythms," and his assignment of a special kind of diction to each of the four "radicals" further articulates the possibilities of generic interpenetration.

The *Anatomy* connects regularly patterned verse with epos, logically straightforward prose with fiction, the verbalization of the stream of a consciousness with lyric, and the permanent suiting of style to the characters and situations of the "internal fiction" with drama. But—if I understand the excessively involved purport of the pertinent passages of the Fourth Essay and *The Well-Tempered Critic* (1963) correctly—Frye considers "the rhythm of recurrence," "the rhythm of continuity," "the rhythm of association," and "the rhythm of decorum" as types of diction most congenial with, yet by no means exclusively constituent of, the respective genres. Understandably enough; for if he were to insist on more closely connecting, for instance, the rhythm of recurrence and *epos* defined as the mimesis of direct address, his fourfold classification would fail to do justice to the complex interplay between writer, hero, and their respective "societies" in most works of literature. As it is, *lyric* and *epos* emerge from the *Anatomy* as predominantly thematic genres with one significant difference between them. Whereas the lyric poet tends to "write as an individual, emphasizing the separateness of his personality and the distinctness of his vision," the writer working in the *epos* form (which includes oratorical prose) devotes himself to being a spokesman of his community; "a poetic knowledge and expressive power which is latent or needed in his society comes to articulation in him" (p. 54). *Fiction* and *drama* are in turn allied in their relative neglect for the thematic relations of "external fiction" between writer and reader. The chief verbal vehicle of fiction is a kind of prose which tends to be a "transparent medium" presenting its subject matter as "plate glass in a shop window" presents what is behind it. Still, Frye readily admits that "fully realized prose" has its own distinctive semantic rhythm with the articulate sentence as its unit (pp. 265, 268; cf. also *The Well-Tempered Critic*, pp. 18, 24). Only the generic rhythm of drama can be described as "epos or fiction absorbed by decorum"—a variety of speech rhythms appropriate to individual speakers in specific situations (p. 269).

Interrelating his concepts of mode and genre, Frye observes the ascendancy of *epos* in myth and romance, followed by the respective predominance of drama, fiction, and lyric in the high-mimetic, low-mimetic, and ironic "periods." The fact that comedy and prose—traditionally associated with the lower ranks—exhibit greater "power of adaptation" to low-mimetic and ironic standards than tragedy and verse *epos* may encourage the assumption of large-scale interdependence between different aspects of Frye's system in most trends of literary history (pp. 269ff). Yet many exceptions could be cited. For example, even though Wordsworth's theory of poetry as differing from prose only in metre but not in diction is a "low mimetic manifesto" (p. 271), Frye himself points out that Romanticism at large made its "thematic" poets appear what the "fictional hero" was in the age of romance—"an extraordinary person who lives in a higher and more imaginative order of experience" than his fellow men (p. 59). In general, inconsistencies in Frye's "Utopian History" only prove that the "scientific" and "evangelical" ambitions inherent in his ideal of criticism have not yet been demonstrably reconciled. (Cf. Angus Fletcher, p. 31, and Geoffrey H. Hartman, pp. 111f.) The vast dimensions and persuasive power of his critical thought still warrant the "suspended judgement" which, as W. K. Wimsatt deplores, critics have been yielding to Frye's often elusive theoretical "apparitions" ("Criticism as Myth," p. 99). Part of Frye's persuasive power originates, I believe, in his resolutely synoptic view of literature. Employing several principles of generic classification instead of subordinating, for example, a concept of tragedy to a concept of drama or *vice versa*, Frye's theory of genre is in the best critical tradition. Not unlike Aristotle's coordinated distinctions according to the means, objects, and manner of *mimesis*, Frye's concepts of *mythoi*, modes, and radicals of presentation help us see literary works within a polycentric conceptual framework.

Despite his apparent delight in highly sophisticated arguments, Frye is on record as saying that "the only guarantee that a subject is theoretically coherent is its ability to have its elementary principles taught to children" (The Developing Imagination," p. 33). Equally challenging is the statement from the Polemical Introduction to the *Anatomy*: "If criticism could ever be conceived as a coherent and systematic study, the elementary principles of which could be explained to any intelligent nineteen-year-old, then, from the point of view of such a conception, no critic now knows the first thing about criticism" (p. 14). Of the many teachers of literature who have engaged in explaining the elementary principles of Frye's criticism to the "intelligent nineteen-year-old," Robert Scholes and Carl H. Klaus should be mentioned here. In a recent series of lucid textbooks, Scholes' *Elements of Fiction* (1968) and *Elements of Poetry* (1969) have been followed by two booklets jointly authored by Scholes and Klaus: *Elements of the Essay* (1969) and *Elements of Drama* (1971). Scholes and Klaus make no reference to any critic, yet their indebtedness to Frye is almost too obvious to require explicit acknowledgment. It is, indeed, deviations from the letter rather than the spirit of Frye's concepts of genre that I shall discuss in the following pages.

Scholes and Klaus attempt to provide a terminology which is more transparent than Frye's own for the basic concepts of the *Anatomy*. Instead of *mythoi* we hear about "fictional modes and patterns." Similarly, Frye's alignment of some phases of comedy and tragedy with irony, and of other phases with romance, gives way to a much simpler system of six fictional modes: the heroic and the antiheroic quest, the tragic and the pathetic fall, and the comic and the satiric rise. Scholes explains that quests involve movement rather than change, and that the change effected by fall or rise is "straightforward" in tragedy and comedy but "ironic" in pathos and satire: as an "initiation into a world of ugliness and disorder" the satiric rise "amounts to corruption," and the pathetic fall of a lowly creature whose doom in a debased world results from his "unfortunate virtue or delicacy" represents a kind of rise. The six modes emerge in relative purity from the "phantasy worlds of romance and satire" whose distortions are "ways of seeing certain aspects of reality more clearly at the expense of others." It is harder to detect the same modes in the sphere of "realism"—a conceptual area roughly corresponding to the low mimetic among Frye's modes of the displacement of myths. Scholes suggests that in realism "neat, schematic distinctions fade; the various patterns combine and interact; and values themselves are called into question: rise and fall, success and failure—all become problematic" (*Fiction*, pp. 10ff). Yet we can always ask ourselves whether the writer of a work "has focused on the beautiful or the ugly, on the orderly or the chaotic," in other words, whether his work is primarily romantic or satiric. Likewise, we can always try to establish whether the initial opposition of the principal characters is at the end replaced by comic harmony or else, on the contrary, the initial harmony between the hero and his world disintegrates so that we finally see the hero in a state of tragic isolation (*Drama*, pp. 43ff). Ignoring in this context the difference between the comic and the satiric rise on the one hand and between the tragic and the pathetic fall on the other, Scholes and Klaus introduce a simple diagram (p. 44) which shows romance and satire emphasizing "the essential qualities" of the world while comedy and tragedy "emphasize the dominant patterns of human experience." With its "absence of emphasis," the point of intersection in turn "refers to the world as it is" (see accompanying diagram*).

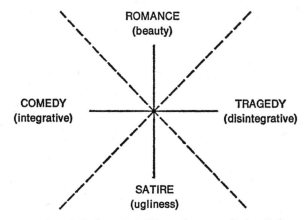

I regret that Scholes and Klaus have refrained from summarizing their implicit interrelation of Frye's *mythoi* and modes in diagrammatic form. It seems appropriate to do so by inserting "realism," the area of fading distinctions, between the highly polarized universe of the imagination and its undifferentiated "center"—the actual world (see accompanying diagram).

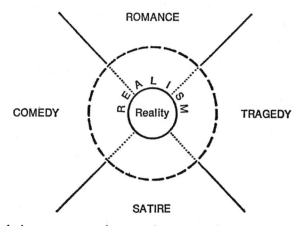

In their most conspicuous departure from the *Anatomy*, Scholes and Klaus substitute the familiar concepts "essay" and "story" for Frye's somewhat elusive distinction between "epos" and "fiction" as "the mimesis of direct address" and "the mimesis of assertive writing." As a result, they arrive at a simpler and more conventional division of literature into essays, stories, plays, and poems. According to the *Elements of the Essay*, those four categories designate "four important points on a continuum of literary possibilities": the author and the reader of an essay are the only characters in this "most direct and utilitarian" of literary forms; the fictive characters of a story come to us "through the voice of a narrator"; in plays we overhear words spoken "publicly" by dramatic characters; and we simply overhear a poem, "the most indirect and esthetic of the forms" (pp. 2f). Two years later Scholes and Klaus suggest a more convincing basis for the same fourfold classification, as they propose to consider "how words are used and communicated" in different types of literary works (*Drama*, pp. 16ff). In plays and stories, words are used to create plots and characters; in essays and poems, they are used to express ideas and feelings. In the "rhetorical situation" of essays and stories, words are directly addressed to the reader; in the "poetic situation" of plays and poems, they are overheard by him. The idea of a "continuum" of genres is thus replaced by a system of coordinates as shown in the diagram (p. 19) reproduced below.*

The obvious simplification of this scheme is mitigated by the significant statement that "within each of the four literary forms all four possibilities exist again as emphases or strategies" (*Essay*, pp. 3f, *Drama*, p. 19). To be sure, Elster, Frye, Ruttkowski, and (in the framework of threefold classifications) several other critics have suggested comparably flexible principles of generic interplay. Yet we seldom find such a consistent application of theory to practice as Scholes and Klaus's discussion of works exemplifying "the essay as essay," "the essay as story," "the essay as play," and "the essay as

* From *Elements of Drama* by Carl Klaus and Robert Scholes. Copyright © 1971 by Oxford University Press, Inc. Reprinted by permission.

poem." In their most recent book they even consider selected passages of plays as leaning toward narration, lyric meditation, or essayistic persuasion. This commendable shift of focus from macrostructure to microstructure highlights a shortcoming in Scholes and Klaus's basic concepts. "Essay," "story," "play," and "poem" refer to the whole rather than the parts of literary works; those categories thus conceal the fact that such a fourfold classification is best applied in the study of what may be called the "molecular structure" of discourse.

The substitution of "essay" and "story" for Frye's "epos" and "fiction" stresses the important difference between predominantly thematic and predominantly fictional literature. The resulting greater clarity seems to me to justify the concomitant disregard for the question whether a given thematic or narrative work primarily adheres to oral or written traditions. What I cannot accept in Scholes and Klaus's modification of Frye's theory of genre is their choice of the essay as the fourth generic prototype. Clearly, generalizations based on this very specialized and relatively late form of literary persuasion will often prove misleading. In oracles and commandments, proverbs and aphorisms, puns and riddles, we are not at all "directly addressed" by a highly individualized speaker such as the implied author of an oratorical essay. The "author" implied by those most persuasive texts is either a god or, so to speak, the wisely playful spirit of language. As I shall argue at greater length in the next chapter, the impersonal yet very artistic type of communication characteristic of the memorable adage and related forms should serve as the conceptual model of thematic persuasion within the realm of imaginative literature. The selection of the essay as the central category corresponding to story, play, and poem is undesirable for at least two reasons. Certain "essays"—most newspaper editorials as well as a good deal of published research, even in the humanities—are examples of nonartistic, purely utilitarian verbal communication; as such, they are not works of imaginative literature at all. Yet whenever an individual persuader's voice becomes enjoyably audible in artistic, "personal" essays, their nature is not strictly thematic any longer. Within the realm of thematic presentation, such essays approach the lyric poet's "enactment" of vision.

Chapter Five

Conclusions and Propositions

1. The Case for Polycentric Classifications

Most readers of this survey will agree that the familiar division of literature into a lyric, a narrative, and a dramatic genre no longer corresponds to the advanced insights of modern genre criticism. That threefold classification may provide the convenient rationale for scheduling a manageable triad of Freshman English courses for many years to come. Yet few instructors (and perhaps even fewer of their best students) are likely to consider the pigeonholes "Poetry," "Fiction," and "Drama" fit to house such larger birds as Eliot's *Waste Land*, Joyce's *Ulysses*, or Faulkner's *Requiem for a Nun*. Even Germany, where the holy trinity of genre criticism became canonized around 1800, shows signs of the coming of a second Reformation. Dissatisfied with such concessions from within the Church as Emil Staiger's reinterpretation of the three genres as three easily combinable generic styles, several scholars have lately presumed to attack the very dogma of the trinity (Boeckh, Sengle). Quite a few of them have indeed decided to revert to a pre-Romantic fourfold classification and suggest adding some version of the "didactic" genre to the revered triad (Flemming, Ruttkowski, Seidler).

The trouble with the reformers is that they move even

further away than the unreformed from the fountainhead of generic classifications—Socrates' distinctions between straightforward presentation (*diegesis*), impersonating re-presentation (*mimesis*), and a mixed style in which poet and characters alternate as speakers (*Republic*, Book Three, 392c and d). Wisely enough, Socrates (or Plato) applied the criterion of "speakers" only to the "style" (as opposed to the "matter") of poetic discourse. Likewise, Aristotle adopted the Platonic categories as relevant to only one—the third—aspect of his interrelated generic distinctions according to the means, the objects, and the manner of *mimesis*. It seems clear that the Greek philosophers' sober principle of discussing literature in a polycentric conceptual framework is preferable to the illusory promise of unity and simplicity held out by most summary classifications. As my survey has been intended to demonstrate, it is not a particular doctrine of three (or four or fourteen) genres that the discerning critic should reject. The fallacy lies in the monistic principle of classification usually underlying such doctrines. We seem to need several systems of coordinates—Northrop Frye's *Anatomy of Criticism* alone employs at least three—lest we lose our way in the more-than-three-dimensional universe of verbal art. There are many respects in which literary works can be similar, and distinctions based on different types of similarities need not be mutually exclusive. Given the slow interaction between most critical approaches of our day, it is an important task of future theories of literature to explore how the best generic concepts propounded in the last few decades may become integrated into a set of interlocking "systems."

The most useful ones among future theories will hardly remain near the poles of what might be called the rhetorical axis of criticism connecting writer and reader through the work. We have seen the great dangers incurred by most "expressive" theories of genre. The reason why those dangers are always imminent is this: even though the assumption that similar works are products of similar minds or similar states of mind is to some extent justified, it is completely hypothetical to discuss generic similarities in terms of what is responsible for them in the authors' minds. (Cf. Beriger, Hartl, Petsch, Spoerri, Wundt.) Projected by Ernest Bovet on the more clearly visible screen of literary history, several familiar expressive tenets fully revealed their abstract, speculative nature. At the other end of the rhetorical axis we find the "pragmatic" critic with his emphasis on the similarity of the effects similar works have on their readers. (Cf. Dohrn, Hamburger, Meyer.) This orientation will yield more reliable insights, since every critic has some firsthand experience of a work's effect on at least one reader—himself. Indeed, even "structural" and "mimetic" critics must start out from such "effects" if they want to inquire into the nature of the "causes." After all, how would anyone know what to investigate, had the works under study not produced certain impressions on his mind? Yet those impressions are best objectified in terms of what produced them—the verbal structure and the mimetic import of literary works.

The relative merits of the "structural" and the "mimetic" approach are more difficult to assess. We must compare them with Aristotle's words in mind: "It is the mark of an educated man to look for precision in each class of things just so far as the nature of the subject admits; it is evidently equally foolish to accept probable reasoning from the mathematician and to demand from the rhetorician scientific proofs" (*Nicomachean Ethics*, Book One, 1094b). Beyond doubt, literary criticism is a field of "probable reasoning." Within its confines, however, some lines of inquiry admit of a greater degree of precision than others. Judging from the theories surveyed here, the modes of literary evocation can, and therefore should, be classified with greater exactitude than the mimetic results of the evocation. Yet the exploration of the latter field—the types of imaginative worlds evoked by literary works—is at least as important as the study of the former—the structural types (or modes) of discourse bringing about the writer's "mimesis."

One reason why structural critics tend to frame more precise genre concepts than their mimetic colleagues is their analytical focus on the parts rather than the wholes of literary works. Ever since Socrates in the third book of Plato's *Republic* distinguished *diegesis, mimesis,* and their combination as three modes of discourse, it has been assumed that a given mode may but does not necessarily inform entire works. The same holds for Aristotle's similarly "structural" distinctions according to the manner of mimesis. In contrast, Aristotle's "mimetic" distinctions according to the objects of mimesis—men "either above our own level of goodness, or beneath it, or just such as we are" (*Poetics*, Chapter Two, 1448a)—rely on macro- rather than microstructure, that is, on works as wholes rather than sums of their parts. To be sure, most "structural" as well as "mimetic" theories of genre propounded or endorsed in the twentieth century are more complex than the Greek tripartitions just cited. Yet the bent to distinguish different modes of discourse in the subsequent parts of one and the same work is still with us, and so is the contrary disposition to characterize entire works as evoking a certain type of imaginative world. Since detached parts can be analysed more precisely than functioning wholes, the usual difference in exactitude between "structural" and "mimetic" theories is comparable to the difference between the respective degrees of precision aimed at by the biologist investigating the brain cells of dissected monkeys and by the behaviorist comparing the learning habits of the animals, whole and alive.

2. *The Modes and Perspectives of Discourse*

An important set of insights, emerging from the structural considerations of (not only structural) critics, invites being clarified and interrelated in diagrammatic form. Harking back to Socrates's remarks on *diegesis* and *mimesis*, we can consider authorial, thematic *presentation* and interpersonal, dramatic *representation* as poles between which, so to speak, the evocative power of verbal discourse is generated and beyond which literature as *verbal art* ceases to exist.[1] Within the realm of imaginative literature so defined, the classification of extreme possibilities should be easy enough. Closest to assertive discourse—the nonartistic verbal presentation of supposedly verifiable facts—we find proverbial formulations of imaginative truth. In this relatively unmixed form, thematic presentation adumbrates some idea without relating it to an event or a speaking voice. For example: "Man proposes, God disposes"; or : "Where there is a will, there is a way." We do not know who speaks the words, to whom they are directed, or from what particular experience the statements

---

[1] Cf. the first paragraph and especially note 1 of the Appendix. The ensuing consideration of the modes and perspectives of discourse is a shortened and revised version of my article, "Verbal Worlds between Action and Vision," College English, XXXIII (1971). Reprinted by permission.

derive their suggested validity. In fact, the two proverbs just quoted verbalize rather conflicting insights. Yet through metaphoric and acoustic poignancy, each succeeds in intimating *pan-orama*—a mental picture of *all* that can be *seen*.

Words spoken in realistic plays are very different; they clearly point to particular speakers, listeners, and circumstances. The beginning of Arthur Miller's *All My Sons* may serve to illustrate this point:

JIM: Where's your tobacco?
KELLER: I think I left it on the table. *Jim goes slowly to table in the arbor, finds a pouch, and sits there on the bench, filling his pipe.* Gonna rain tonight.
JIM: Paper says so?
KELLER: Yeah, right here.
JIM: Then it can't rain.

Both the dialogue and the stage directions of conversational drama invite *panto-mime*—total representation of a specific interpersonal action. One further step away from authorial presentation and we enter the sphere of wordless pantomine —the artistic but nonverbal representation of action.

Adage and conversational dialogue are, of course, not the only thematic and dramatic modes of literary discourse. Yet in other modes of presentation and representation, the authorial point of view of timeless mental vision and the fictive interpersonal point of view of a concrete temporal action interact more perceptibly. The characters in allegorical plays and philosophical dialogues speak and act on behalf of ideas whose validity they have been evoked to demonstrate; for example, the rudimentary action of *Everyman* or Plato's *Symposium* suggests the interpersonal perspective of fictive characters only to subordinate it to the thematic framework of authorial vision. The interplay of thematic presentation and dramatic representation is more intricate in Aesop's or La Fontaine's fables or in Kafka's parable "Before the Law" (whether we read it as an independent story or as part of the cathedral chapter of *The Trial*). Such narrative pieces delineate characters and events that are lively enough in their own fictional right, yet the explicit or implicit moral of the story will emerge—or vexingly conceal itself—as the given text's supreme organizing principle. (Cf. Crane, Elster, Kleiner, Olson.) Likewise, direct appeals to the reader suggest an engaged speaker's voice without shifting the emphasis, as lyric texts do, from the universal content to the private act of communication. This holds not only for artistic oratory and the oratorical passages of certain essays. The narrator of short stories and novels may similarly permit his "private" perspective to inform some of his words:

Dear reader! It rests with you and me whether, in our two fields of action, similar things shall be or not. Let them be! We shall sit with lighter bosoms on the hearth, to see the ashes of our fires turn grey and cold.

[Dickens, *Hard Times*, Book Three, Chapter Nine]

Adage, expository or allegoric dialogue, fable or parable, and direct appeal to a listening or reading audience are, then, four distinct modes of predominantly authorial presentation. In contrast, an interpersonal perspective internal to the represented action informs the bulk of the dialogue in the majority of plays. As Joyce had young Stephen Dedalus put it in Chapter Five of *A Portrait*, the dramatic artist, "like the God of the creation, remains within or behind or beyond or above his handiwork, invisible, refined out of existence, paring his fingernails." Surely, the playwright can do all those things; but (as Roman Ingarden's, Una Ellis-Fermor's Peter Szondi's, and Volker Klotz's pertinent remarks imply) he does not have to. The Greek chorus and certain types of dramatic figures (messengers, prophets, mouthpiece characters) often contribute to the dialogue thematic aspects which its inter-subjective internal perspective does not warrant: Cassandra predicts and the Chorus contemplates Agamemnon's fate before Aeschylus allows us to hear the King's death cry from the inside of the palace. Such interference with the irreversible and even temporal flux of a represented action is closely related to flashbacks, anticipatory remarks, and other devices which make a dual mode of orientation—the simultaneous relevance of authorial and figural perspectives—prevail in most works of narrative fiction. A comparable residue of the authorial vision penetrates the utterances of dramatic figures through another channel whenever they reveal subconversa-tional or even subconscious depths of their minds. Being private, those depths must be communicated to the reader or spectator of a play in one of two ways: either "above the heads" of the other characters through the stylized diction of poetic drama, or in the almost entirely lyric medium of soliloquies. In either case, the speaker's quasi-lyric, private perspective informs his words insofar as they function as ve-hicles of self-expression rather than means of interpersonal communication. Authorial prologues, epilogues, the stage di-rections of printed plays, and the familiar narrator figure of modern drama are in turn frankly presentational, quasi-thematic ingredients in the dramatic representation of an action. We may visualize the relationship between the modes of thematic and dramatic discourse as shown in the accompanying diagram.

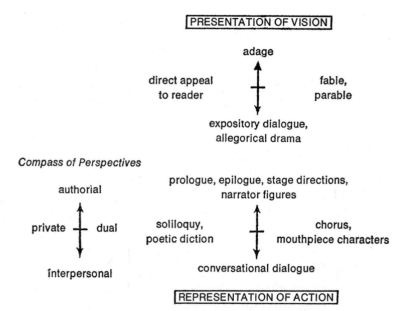

So far we have considered verbal structures in which action or vision prevails to a marked degree. To be sure, didactic fable and choral commentary employ quasi-narrative modes of discourse which to some extent rely on a dual point of view. Yet only the typical modes of narrative fiction succeed fully in combining the authorial perspective of vision and the fictive interpersonal perspective of action into the dual focus of *envisioned action*. (Cf. Friedemann, Hartl, Hirt, Meyer.) Due to their considerable length, most narrative works keep shifting their emphasis between presentation and representation—authorial "telling" and impersonating "showing." (Cf. Booth, Fernandez, N. Friedman, Ingarden, Lubbock, Ludwig, Stanzel.) For the most part, however, they neither present vision nor represent action but provide what may be described as the presentation of action. This can be illustrated with reference to Tolstoy's *Anna Karenina*, quoted here in David Magarshack's translation from the Signet Classic paperback. The first sentence of the novel presents an insight in the abstract thematic mode of the *adage*:

A) All happy families are like one another; each unhappy family is unhappy in its own way.

The next paragraph abandons the mode of thematic panorama, but it is still from a panoramic bird's-eye perspective that it begins to *survey* the spatial and temporal setting of the narrated events:

B) Everything was in confusion in the Oblonsky household. The wife had found out that the husband had had an affair with the French governess and had told him that she could not go on living in the same house with him. This situation had now gone on for three days and was felt acutely by the husband and wife themselves, by all members of the family, and by their servants.

Soon enough, the narrator directs his "camera" at a clearly defined, particular *scene*:

C) On the third morning after the quarrel Prince Stephan Arkedyevich Oblonsky (Stivy, as he was called by his society friends) woke up at his usual time, that is at eight o'clock, not in his wife's bedroom but on the morocco leather sofa in his study. He turned his plump, well-cared-for body on the well-sprung sofa, as though intending to go to sleep for a long time, hugged the pillow on the other side, and pressed his cheek against it. Suddenly he jumped up, sat down on the sofa, and opened his eyes.

The attentive reader of this passage cannot help but adopt its radically dual perspective: even though he is "listening" to a narrator, he is also "experiencing" the narrated action through the consciousness of one of the fictive participants. As a result, he is prepared to receive and appreciate an *inside view* of Oblonsky's slowly awakening mind:

> D) "Yes, yes, now how was it?" he thought, trying to remember a dream. "Yes, now how was it? Oh, yes! Alabin was giving a dinner in Darmstadt; no, not in Darmstadt but in some American city. Ah, but in my dream Darmstadt was in America. Yes, Alabin was giving a dinner on glass tables. . . ."

Shortly afterwards, we are made to witness an event from the most consistently dual point of view [2] narrative fiction can provide; action is being envisioned by a fictive character for whose thoughts and remembered perceptions the narrator nevertheless *substitutes* his own words:

> E) "Dear, oh dear!" he kept saying in despair, recalling the most painful aspects of the quarrel. The most unpleasant moment was the first, when, having returned from the theater happy and gay, with an enormous pear in his hand for his wife, he had not found her in the drawing room. Nor, to his amazement, did he find her in the study. At last he had discovered her in the bedroom with the unfortunate note in her hand that disclosed everything. Dolly, whom he always thought of as preoccupied, busy, and not very intelligent, was sitting motionless, holding the note in her hands, and looked at him with an expression of horror, despair, and anger. "What is this? This?" she asked, pointing to the note.

In the next chapter, finally, Tolstoy almost reaches the *dramatic* mode of representation as he renders figural speech

[2] Cf. Appendix: "Free Indirect Discourse and Related Techniques."

with a minimum of intervention on the part of the narrator:

> F) "Don't worry, sir," said Matvey. "It'll all come right."
> "Come right?"
> "Yes, sir."
> "You think so?"

Surely, Tolstoy employed thematic (A) and panoramic (B) modes of discourse more extensively in *War and Peace*, and other novelists made more radical use of interior monologue (D), substitutionary narration (E), and dialogue (F). But the selections from *Anna Karenina* demonstrate how naturally a versatile writer can combine scenic narration (C) with thematic (A), quasi-thematic (B), quasi-lyric (D), pronouncedly dual (E), and quasi-dramatic (F) modes of discourse.

Lyric texts being usually shorter than works of narrative fiction, we should not expect individual poems to oscillate between different modes of discourse to the same extent. Quite to the contrary, poems as well as markedly lyric texts in prose tend to adhere to the same mode of evocation throughout. But how, exactly, do such verbal structures evoke their "worlds"? The difficulty involved in finding a general answer to that question is obviously great, yet, perhaps, not insurmountable. (Cf. Wellek.) I hope to look in the right direction for such an answer by proposing to ascribe to the lyric a complex rather than simple generic principle— the principle of integrating the "timeless" quality of thematic vision with the intersubjective temporal progress of dramatic action into the private time and perspective of *enacted vision*. In this respect the contrast between proverbial and lyric texts is very illuminating. While adages merely imply a mind that has arrived at clearly evoked insights, the lyric poet evokes the inner voice of a man now striving to verbalize whatever may emerge from the "existential" depth of his conscious or subconscious psyche. (Cf. Burke, Frye, Hamburger, Jakobson, Joyce, Lukács, Staiger.)

Four main types of lyric structure stand out in the great variety of poetic genres. Quasi-thematic meditative poems stress the speaker's vision as something to be communicated to the reader. Quasi-dramatic monologues (for example, Robert Browning's "My Last Duchess" or Goethe's "Zauber-lehrling") emphasize the speaker's situation and past or present actions in relation to other fictive characters. Focusing on the private experience of the very act of vision, songlike poems often maintain a nearly perfect balance between a theme (usually describable as a mood) and the evoked circumstances of its verbal representation. In this most consistently integrated phase the lyric enactment of vision even "throws a shadow," as Longinus said of the sublime orator's rhetorical devices, over the writer's art, keeping the devices as such concealed from the esthetically contemplating reader. What results is the illusion that we are overhearing an inner voice speaking or rather singing in an almost involuntary manner; Wordsworth's "A Slumber Did My Spirit Seal" and Goethe's "Mailied" are well-known examples. No such clearly personified source as the "singer" of lyric songs animates the quasi-narrative enactment of vision through the objective correlatives of a theme or mood. (Cf. Barthes, Eliot, Walzel.) Yet many ballads and a good deal of baroque and modern poetry exemplify that the lyric voice may primarily present *itself* by narrating a story (George Herbert, "The Collar"), describing an inner scene (Paul Valéry, "In-térieur"), or delineating a meditative emblem, as in Erich Fried's "Adam":

> Bild aus Ton
> Atem eingetan

zu tönendem Tun
und wieder gelähmt
zu Lehm[3]

Such ostensibly impersonal and detached poetry yields itself readily to analytical discussion in new-critical terms like
William Empson's "ambiguity," Robert Penn Warren's
"irony," or Cleanth Brooks's "paradox." Since this mode of
lyric evocation was particularly favored and perfected by
Rimbaud, Mallarmé, and their twentieth-century disciples,
we should not be surprised that it induced a French critic,
Jean-Paul Sartre, to frame a concept of *poésie* at large as
consisting of impersonal, largely noncommunicative "word-
objects." Of course, Emil Staiger's account of the lyric
attitude as a poet's almost involuntary self-expression is likewise one-sided: it reflects the decisive influence of the songlike masterpieces of Goethe, Eichendorff, Brentano, and a
few other romanticists on the majority of critics in the German tradition. Taking several kinds of lyric poetry into account, we may liken most of its ways of evoking an inner
voice to a painter's production of self-portraits. Rembrandt's
self-portraits, for example, tell us what kind of painter, not
what kind of man, he was. The most personal thing we may
hope to find out is what kind of man a painter—or lyric
poet—wished to appear.

In keeping with the above synopsis of recent structural
thoughts, one *could* say that verbal art evokes imaginative
worlds in four fundamentally different ways: thematic works

[3] From *gedichte* by Erich Fried, Claassen Verlag, Düsseldorf, 1958.
Reprinted by permission. The following translation cannot convey the
ambiguity of the German words *Ton* (clay but also sound) and *tönend*
(resounding but also shading a color): "Image made of clay / breath
infused / for resounding deeds / and lamed again / to be loam."

present, poems enact vision; plays represent, narratives make us envision action. More important than such a gross classification of "genres" is, however, the critic's constant awareness of the fact that several principles of poetic evocation operate in each and every literary work. (Cf. Eliot, Frye, Kayser, Petersen, Ruttkowski, Staiger, Scholes/Klaus.) A certain amount of simplification notwithstanding, the accompanying chart * may help clarify the extent to which the perspectives

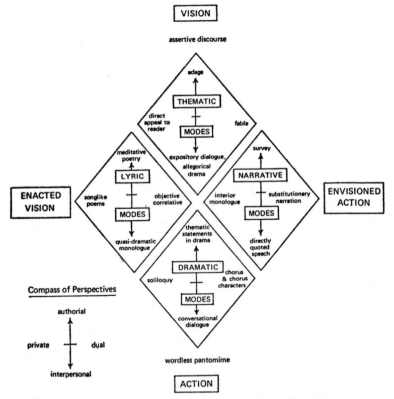

* Reprinted by permission of the National Council of Teachers of English, from Paul Hernadi, "Verbal Worlds between Action and Vision," *College English* (October, 1971), p. 24.

of action, vision, envisioned action, and enacted vision inform different modes of poetic discourse.

Needless to say, the sixteen or so modes I have tried to interrelate indicate tendencies without exhausting all possibilities of poetic discourse. For the sake of greater precision we could amplify the diagram by introducing intermediate categories between the "cornerstones" of the conceptual edifice erected here. Meditative odes or hymns addressing a god or a human being other than the reader would find their place between quasi-thematic and quasi-dramatic poems somewhere around the middle of the lyric square. The scenic narration of gestures (for example, "suddenly he jumped up, sat down on the sofa, and opened his eyes") occupies a similarly central position among narrative modes: it shares such grammatical features as the past-tense and third-person form of reporting with the panoramic survey, yet its abreast perspective on the narrated events resembles the quasi-dramatic temporal orientation of directly quoted speech. The same sphere of envisioned action further includes several familiar techniques of narration between the anonymous, quasi-thematic survey and the highly personal, quasi-lyric interior monologue: stories can be related by the inspired bard, by the collector of allegedly historical documents, by the humble witness of great events, by the reminiscing hero writing his memoirs or diary, and finally (as in Salinger's *Catcher in the Rye*) by the hero as the supposedly oral teller of his emotionally charged tale. In the area of represented action, Tom Wingfield's asides to the audience in Tennessee Williams's *Glass Menagerie* leave the quasi-thematic stance of detached narrators in the direction of quasi-lyric soliloquies; the "epic" Singer of Brecht's *Caucasian Chalk Circle* is in turn a kind of first chorister among his Four Musicians.

Rather than elaborate on further details, I hasten to add that the modes of discourse are not always clearly distinguishable. It depends on the critic's approach to *Gulliver's Travels* whether he should consider it a didactic fable, a fictive autobiography, or a combination of the two. But he may choose to contrast some pasages, chapters, or even books of the work as predominantly thematic to others as predominantly fictional. In so doing, he will endorse rather than invalidate the microstructural theory of poetic discourse suggested here.

This theory is based on the observation that imaginative literature relies on a more or less balanced interplay of verbal presentation and artistic representation. As soon as the presentation of vision or the representation of action unduly prevails in a literary work we feel that we could and perhaps should apply categories other than literary for its proper evaluation. Thus we may wish to probe the truth content of adages or the theatrical effectiveness of naturalistic plays even though we realize that we have not left the field of verbal art behind while contemplating those predominantly thematic or dramatic verbal constructs. To be sure, nonartistic discourse and nonverbal pantomime lie outside the realm of imaginative literature. Even they contain, however, at least a modicum of both action and vision, since all verbal presentation involves the interpersonal action of speaking or writing, and all representation in turn involves selection and point of view betraying authorial vision. Only if we follow the vertical axis of the chart beyond assertive discourse in one direction and beyond wordless pantomime in the other, shall we approach the purest forms of vision and action postulated by the human imagination: the timeless, serene panorama of *logos* and the perpetual, teeming pantomime of *physis*.

The other arts, those less forbidding subjects for the literary critic, loom along the continuation of the horizontal axis of literature. Evoking moods—private patterns of the imagination—rather than universal insights or intersubjective actions, songlike poems resemble actual songs, the most "literary" works of music. On the other hand, the consistently dual perspective of substitutionary narration finds an analogy in the "dual" art of the cinema adding the authorial camera's varying angles and distances or sometimes even a speaker's running commentary to the filmed events. Go further in either direction and, having abandoned the semiverbal areas of songs and sound films, you reach the realm of productive design (music, architecture, and other "abstract" arts) on the side of enacted vision, and the reproductive visual arts (first silent movies, then objective sculpture, painting, and photography) beyond the literary sphere of envisioned action.

Finding our way back to literature, it will not surprise us that the respective share of action and vision in a literary work determines which aspects of its world are vividly evoked, and which aspects merely implied, to the imagination of the attentive reader. Thematic presentation leaves innumerable details unmentioned. "Where there is a will, there is a way"—this proverb evokes an insight without evoking any concrete manifestation of its suggested truth. The quasi-thematic sentence, "Everything was in confusion in the Oblonsky household," is far less general; such an instance of the panoramic survey still implies rather than evokes human beings in action. Consider now the beginning of the second act from Oscar Wilde's *The Importance of Being Earnest:*

> MISS PRISM (calling): Cecily, Cecily! Surely such utilitarian occupation as the watering of flowers is rather Moulton's duty than yours? Especially at a moment when intellectual pleasures await you. Your German grammar is on the table. Pray open it at page fifteen. We will repeat yesterday's lesson.
>
>   . . .
>
> CECILY (coming over very slowly): But I don't like German. It isn't at all a becoming language. I know perfectly well that I look quite plain after my German lesson.

Without looking at the stage or having read the stage direction that describes the scene, we are prompted by the quoted words to visualize many details of Miss Prism's and Cecily's behavior and surroundings. Since, however, an interpersonal perspective strictly internal to the represented action prevails in the conversation, it implies rather than evokes what may be called its universal import—something like "romantic girls prefer flowers to German grammar." Indeed, the limitations of "pure" panorama and "pure" pantomime would be similar to the limitations of symbolic logic and behavioristic psychology: if literature did not always imply more than it evokes, only schematic skeletons of the "whole truth and nothing but the truth" could emerge from its verbal presentation, and only intersubjective, "publicly verifiable" aspects of human life could enter its photostatic *mimesis*. In practice, of course, words in literary works connote much more than they denote. This enables all modes of poetic discourse to make simultaneous use of the abstract, universalizing capacity of presentation and the concrete, particularizing power of representation.

3. *The Scope and Mood of Verbal Worlds*

Our brief consideration of relationships between literature, the other arts, philosophy, and psychology has made us enter a field in which the study of the *modes of literary evocation* must turn into the study of its results—the *imaginative worlds literary works evoke.* Failure to distinguish the proper objectives of the "structural" and the "mimetic" line of inquiry has often resulted in discussions of the lyric, epic, and dramatic "form" in terms of some lyric, epic, and dramatic "spirit." There are legitimate affinities between the findings of "structural" and "mimetic" critics. But the discernment of affinities should not prompt us to abandon the search for a polycentric conceptual framework within which the "molecular" structure of a literary work is clearly distinguished from its overall shape. (Cf. Adorno, Bonnet, Elster, Guérard, Jolles, Kleiner.)

"Shape" is no doubt a metaphor as far as literature is concerned. Yet circumference and color, two primary connotations of the word, suggest two significant aspects of the worlds evoked by verbal art. These are scope and mood: the "size" of the evoked world and the general tone or atmosphere prevailing in it. An esthetically relevant concept of scope will not rely, of course, on the number of words an author puts into his work. Rather, it should refer to the cohesive capacity of the work to integrate the world evoked by those words into an ordered pattern. To achieve such mimetic cohesion is one of the principal tasks of writers, and surely not an easy one; every text is limited both in length and in its range of connotation, yet the imaginative world couched in this "fragmentary" medium of verbal discourse should impress the reader as a self-sufficient whole without noticeable gaps and edges. (Cf. Ingarden, Meyer.) In a sense we expect the literary artist to do what older schools of criticism called improving upon nature rather than simply imitating her: he is to fuse the manageability of the finite with the width and depth of the infinite. As Henry James put it in the preface to *Roderick Hudson:* "Really, universally, relations stop nowhere, and the exquisite problem of the artist is eternally but to draw, by a geometry of his own, the circle in which they shall happily *appear* to do so."

In the visual arts, James's magic circle is usually drawn by the painter's or photographer's skillful handling of the relationship between foreground and background. The writer's verbal evocation of imaginative worlds is partly analogous to the *mimesis* of representational painting. With this analogy in mind (and following hints of Elder Olson, Emil Staiger, Yurij Tynjanov, and especially Georg Lukács), one could evolve a resolutely "mimetic" classification of literary scope. Distinguishing three types of relationship between the fore- and background of verbal worlds, such a classification may provide a new and useful context for certain implications of "expressive," "pragmatic," and "structural" tripartitions as well.

It is characteristic of shorter lyric poems to go without much background. Who knows or wants to know the name, size, and colors of the forest—if, indeed, it *is* a forest—where Goethe's wanderer "sings" his second *Nachtlied:*

> Über allen Gipfeln
> Ist Ruh,
> In allen Wipfeln
> Spürest du
> Kaum einen Hauch;

Die Vögelein schweigen im Walde.
Warte nur, balde
Ruhest du auch.[4]

All we expect and happily receive from the poem is the vivid evocation of a mood prevailing in a human mind. Everything else—even the man to whom that mood can be ascribed—remains hidden in the "unlit" background of the poem. This conspicuous predominance of foreground results in the evocation of a world with the high experiential intensity of *concentric* tension. Our attention is directed to the metaphoric depth rather than the communicatory width of verbal meaning. To the responsive reader's imagination, *Gipfel* evokes more than the concrete physical height of mountain peaks, and *Ruh* does not simply mean the lack of any noise or movement perceived by the senses. But few readers will wonder how long and why the wanderer has been away from home, or just when and where he will find the rest he promises himself in the last two lines of the poem. There is, so to speak, a definitive frame of silence around the text—an impenetrable vacuum around the world—of such concentric works of lyric literature.

Proverbs, too, neutralize the background from which their message emerges. Only because we cannot conceive of speech without speakers—conveyed meaning without a conveyer of meaning—do we assume that someone coined the words "Man proposes, God disposes" before we could ever hear or read them. But no further exploration of the assumed speaker's

---

[4] Here is a translation of this most untranslatable poem: "Over all the peaks / there is rest, / in all the treetops / you feel / hardly a breeze; / the little birds are silent in the forest / Just wait, soon / you will be resting too."

identity is called for: our attention is turned toward the timeless result rather than the temporal progress of verbal formulation. Indeed, adages simulate even more successfully than lyric poems the self-contained completeness of a single experience emerging from its dim "background"—the continuous flux of mental life.

Since proverbs and genuinely "lyric" poems evoke one significant moment or a closely related sequence of moments in the subjective time of a consciousness, they tend to be short and to employ stylistic devices like rhyme, alliteration, refrain, and metaphor. Such devices rely on close interaction between the words of a text. They demand internal correlation rather than external elucidation and, as a result, focus the reader's mind on a single experience as something complete in itself. Yet not only poems and adages evoke verbal worlds characterized by concentric tension. Certain kinds of rational and emotive experience lend themselves readily to dramatization. Dramatic allegory, so-called lyric drama (Maeterlinck's and Yeats's one-act plays, for example), and a good deal of the theater of the absurd clearly focus on experienced situation rather than evolving action. The world of such works is thus informed by concentric tension: not a unified action but a self-contained experiential response to some aspect of the *conditio humana* provides them with a sense of wholeness and unity. Despite the considerable difference in length, the generic scope of these kinds of drama is similar to the scope of adages and poems; it is therefore comparable to the scope—not, of course, to the actual size—of certain still lifes, portraits, and self-portraits with a dim and relatively unimportant background.

Most plays, of course, evoke imaginative worlds sustained by a solid frame of closely interrelated causes and effects—

the so-called unity of action. The events in works like *Antigone* or *Othello* seem to speed toward a predestined point of final rest as if they were subject to some irresistible *kinetic* law of human action. The tightly knit plot of many plays and such lesser narratives as anecdotes, fairy tales, and short stories thus conveys a sense of ineluctable causation and helps evoke the world of such works as a separate, or at least easily and naturally detachable, segment of the universe. As a result, questions like L. C. Knights's ironic "How Many Children Had Lady Macbeth?" are often intriguing yet seldom relevant to the critical elucidation of works of this type; we are provoked to force our mental eyes but not really permitted to see beyond the confines of the world Shakespeare's tragedy more or less explicitly evokes. With regard to the visual arts, this type of scope can be likened to a balanced pictorial relationship between fore- and background, that is to say, to the mimetic scope of interior scenes in which the walls of a room or of a cave impose well-defined natural limits upon the viewer's range of vision.

In order to intensify the kinetic tension of their works, playwrights and short-story writers often compress their imaginative worlds into such small natural units as one family, one day, one city. This explains why neoclassical critics of drama would insist on the famous "unities" of action, place, and time. Yet many great plays and short stories display only one unity—the unity of action—as they focus on a hero's radical "change of fortune" (Aristotle) or one "unheard-of event" (Goethe) involving a small group of main characters. Such unity of action—the manifest causal interconnection between all significant parts of the evoked world—imparts the suspense of "drama" to a work whether or not it employs dramatic or quasi-dramatic modes of evocation. Indeed, narrative works with the kinetic scope of a streamlined, "dramatic" action often motivate the limitations they impose on the reader's vision by recourse to first-person narration. Just like the interpersonal perspective of dialogue, the private point of view of the protagonist, a witness, or any second-hand retailer of noteworthy events helps the writer dissolve his "panorama," the way he sees everything, in the presented or re-presented action. But there is no obligatory relationship between a certain type of perspective and a certain type of scope or tension. Omniscient narration prevails in most ballads, fairy tales, and many short stories including the celebrated *Novellen* of Heinrich von Kleist, yet the world of those works is informed by a pervasive unity of action.

A third type of cohesive capacity or tension is most conspicuous in the large narrative forms: both the great epic poem and the fully fledged novel tend to evoke verbal worlds with potentially unobstructed horizons. Yet the same prevalence of vastly inclusive vision over a significant moment of experience or a single line of overpowering action characterizes poems like Pope's *Essay on Man* or Eliot's *Waste Land* and plays like Goethe's *Faust* or Ibsen's *Peer Gynt* as well. Of course, the limitations inherent in verbal discourse do not cease to operate when it comes to those full-scale approximations not of any particular action but of human vision. We could compile an endless list of what has been "left out" of the ostensibly total world of such *ecumenic* works as the *Iliad*, *War and Peace*, and the complete Judeo-Christian Bible. At the same time, each of those "great books" evokes a world with a fully open, potentially infinite mimetic horizon. The analogy between ecumenic scope in literature and in landscape painting (where the range of the evoked space seems to be determined by the viewer's range of vision) is too obvious to be dwelt upon.

Many verbal worlds with ecumenic tension intimate the cosmic dimensions of their unlimited background by a powerful appeal to the totality of the beholder's vision. This is the case, for instance, in Dante's *Divina commedia* or the Hungarian Imre Madách's far less well known *Tragedy of Man* (1861), an ambitious dramatization of world history. But the "episodic" digressions of plot and poetic thought similarly supersede any actual or apparent unity of action in such less conspicuously vision-oriented works as the *Iliad* or *Faust*. Small wonder that Friedrich Schlegel, one of the most acute early theoreticians of the novel, demanded that intellectual coherence rather than dramatic unity prevail in works belonging to this "romantic" and "universal" genre. The fundamental difference between kinetic and ecumenic scope becomes clear as we turn to cyclic works containing more than one change of fortune or unheard-of event. Just as any work with ecumenic tension contains what seeems to be sufficient "raw material" for several kinetic ones, the sequential arrangement of a certain number of kinetic works often results in establishing the more inclusive framework of ecumenic vision. The reader of Shakespeare's interrelated history plays, Boccaccio's *Decameron*, or Aeschylus's *Oresteia* trilogy, for example, may gain access to an "ecumenic" view of the world through a given series of "kinetic" actions.

Surely, the scope of many works combines aspects of the ecumenic tension of vision, the kinetic tension of action, and the concentric tension of the act of vision. Yet one of those basic types of mimetic cohesion tends to prevail in the macrostructural organization of verbal worlds to a marked degree. In principle, it is either through an intense unit of significant experience, or through an irreversible process of radical change, or else through a potentially total view of human existence that the mood of frustration or fulfillment pervades literary works.

Needless to say, this polar classification of moods—frustration *versus* fulfillment—must be understood as independent of judgments concerning esthetic value. After all, our reactions to works of the representational arts are often "mixed" in a remarkable way. The admirer of Picasso's *Guernica* or Shakespeare's *King Lear* does not really "approve" of what he sees or reads; his esthetic pleasure is largely due to the structured intensity of his frustrated desire that the world evoked by the painting or the play be otherwise. Conversely, our esthetic rejection of "daubed-on beauty" and "tacked-on happy end" stems precisely from the embarrassing sense of unearned wish fulfillment. It is clear, therefore, that the world of an objective painting or literary work can please or displease us in addition, or even in contrast, to our positive or negative response to it as an esthetic object. In partial agreement with concepts of tragedy and comedy suggested by Albert Cook, Ronald S. Crane, Northrop Frye, Susanne K. Langer, Elder Olson, and Emil Staiger, I consider a work tragic if it frustrates, and comic if it gratifies, the fictive aspirations with which its reader is made to identify himself. Certain remarks of Eric Bentley, Karl S. Guthke, and Henry A. Myers in turn point to a tragicomic mood describable as simultaneous frustration and fulfillment.

Such broad concepts of the tragic, comic, and tragicomic mood no doubt encompass more than three types of stage plays: tragedy, comedy, and tragicomedy. There is no reason why a proverb, a lyric poem, a fairy tale, or a novel could not convey one of the three moods; just like plays, they evoke imaginative worlds in which the reader would either wish or not wish to exist, or else toward which his attitudes are ambivalent. Since, however, most plays focus on a "change of fortune" and contrast a happy or unhappy ending to an initially very different situation, the mood emanating from the world of such works is especially pervasive. This is the reason why comedy and tragedy, the most obviously kinetic genres, have long been privileged to lend their names to classifiers and interpreters of nondramatic literature also. The monk's "definition" of tragedy in the *Canterbury Tales* and Fielding's description of *Joseph Andrews* as a "comic epic poem in prose" are widely known early examples, but modern criticism (just as our conversational idiom) constantly extrapolates the nouns "tragedy" and "comedy" and the adjectives "tragic" and "comic" from their original context, the history and theory of the drama.

From the point of view of a mimetic theory of the tragic and the comic as contrary moods, the extrapolation is useful. It permits us to cover the entire distance between complete affirmation and complete rejection as extreme responses to the intellectual and emotional challenge of verbal worlds. With respect to reality, either extreme would be infantile, and a combination of the two responses to the same challenge may even be a symptom of schizophrenia. Both the extremes and their integration are, however, legitimate when they indicate that a reader's esthetic sensibility has responded to a literary artist's tragic, comic, or tragicomic evocation of human action and vision.

In this respect it may be useful to compare the disparate responses elicited by two well-known plays. Why is the world of *Othello* opposed as something that should not be and the world of *Twelfth Night* welcomed as precisely "what you will"? Because the former frustrates and the latter gratifies the aspirations Shakespeare has led us to endorse. To some extent we may empathize with all characters of imaginative literature, as they are, so to speak, our fellow human beings. At the same time, we have our preferences and gladly exchange a Malvolio's frustration for the happiness of the young lovers. Also, we wish that the frustration of Iago's desires were less belated and thus more complete. Yet Othello's hidden insecurity and misapplied distrust, partly due to his precarious position as an outsider in the social fabric of Venice, counteract from within the noble Moor's desire for relaxed happiness; it is of Desdemona's adultery, not of her innocence, that he demands, and is later convinced to have received, "ocular proof" (Act 3, Scene 3). In other words, the world of *Othello* is such that the desires with which we are made to identify in it must be frustrated for reasons more profound than Iago's villainous machinations. This raises the play above the level of sentimental melodrama. Likewise, *Twelfth Night* rises above the level of punitive farce through its emphasis—*not* on Malvolio's petty frustrations but on his antagonists' delight in a world designed to grant them eventual happiness. Compared to melodrama and farce, tragedy and comedy can thus be seen as more fully developed, "larger" vehicles of the tragic and the comic mood. Frustration or fulfillment appear accidental in the worlds of melodrama and farce; they emerge as highly plausible, if not indeed necessary, in fully fledged tragedy and comedy.

Clearly, the general tone of frustration or fulfillment can prevail in nondramatic works as well—consider Blake's "London" and Flaubert's *Madame Bovary* on the one hand, Tennyson's "Crossing the Bar" and Fielding's *Tom Jones* on the other. Even adages or at least a large number of familiar proverbs may be regarded as fundamentally comic or tragic in this sense of the word. The world implied by the proverb, "Where there is a will, there is a way," is totally susceptible to human desires. In the absence of explicit indications to the contrary, we assume that life in such a world is desirable. "Man proposes, God disposes"—the world implied by this no less "valid" proverb is governed by a much more dignified principle than the will of men and women. It is still a world fraught with tragedy for a simple reason: not a cosmic purpose but the experiential reality of human fulfillment or frustration determines the mood of texts with a concentric tension.

Frustration and wish fulfillment, be it the writer's, the hero's, or the reader's, have attracted much attention in modern criticism. Indeed, Freud's insistence on the gap between human desires (*Wunschprinzip*) and the potential of the universe to satisfy them (*Realitätsprinzip*) impressed many critics to the point of slighting literary works from which, as the normal way of the world, a sense of lasting happiness emerges. Another group of critics including Northrop Frye would conversely interpret the triumphant end phase of natural and spiritual rebirth myths as suggesting that the ultimate fulfillment of human desires is a higher principle of reality than Freud's *Realitätsprinzip*. I find Frye's subsumption of the noblest, partly indeed other-worldly human desires under an expanded concept of the Pleasure Principle very stimulating. (Cf. A Natural Perspective, pp. 123f.) On strictly literary evidence, however, I would rather abstain from taking sides in the seesaw of fulfillment and frustration. To express my view in the myth critic's own terms: the "natural cycle" of the seasons does not terminate in spring or summer any more than it terminates in fall or winter. As Susanne K. Langer's unbiased juxtaposition of the comic and the tragic "rhythm" implies, literature as a whole suggests that the tragicomic seesaw of life and death, pleasure and pain, victory and defeat, fulfillment and frustration is the "principle" of human reality.

The following conclusions may be justified concerning the imaginative worlds that literary works evoke. While the *intended totality of vision* sustains ecumenic works, and the *self-supporting unity of action* provides a more solid yet smaller framework for kinetic ones, the *experienced identity of action and vision* in the evoked or implied act of mental vision unifies verbal worlds with concentric tension. Works characterized by any of the three tensional types may be predominantly tragic, comic, or tragicomic. From concentric works fulfillment, frustration, or a combination of both emerge as *significant moments* of human experience. The kinetic scope of most plays and many shorter narratives evokes worlds in which the fulfillment and frustration of human desires assume the character of a *temporal process*. Ecumenic works in turn encompass tragic as well as comic moments and processes in manifold combinations, thus creating the impression of *potential totality;* not everything is, but everything could be, included within the scope of their unobstructed horizon.

Whereas concentric works usually abide in the zone of fulfillment or frustration and kinetic works tend to suggest radical change in terms of the hero's ascent or descent, the typical ecumenic work will not permit either mood to become more than slightly prevalent at the expense of the other. Of course, exceptions can be found. Yet our tendency to interpret adages and lyric poems as expressive manifestations of either fulfillment or frustration reveals the difficulty involved in effectively compressing both moods into the small compass of concentric tension. By contrast, melodrama, farce, idyllic romance, and related types of works combining kinetic or ecumenic intentions with a limited, exclusively tragic or comic mood of vision, tend to preclude the mature reader's "willing suspension of disbelief." There is too little likeness between his circumspect view of reality and the worlds of despair beyond hope, or of merriment without fear, that such works attempt to evoke.

Given the important differences between the three types of scope or tension, it is not surprising that works belonging to different types integrate comic and tragic moods in different ways. Concentric texts like Kafka's "Up in the Gallery" or Wordsworth's Lucy poem, "A Slumber Did My Spirit Seal," contain frustration and fulfillment in the form of an inextricable thematic *dichotomy;* comparable to equations with two possible values for an unknown X, such concentric works invite predominantly tragic or comic interpretations according to the interpreter's frame of reference. The tragic and comic aspects of the Misanthrope's exodus from human society or (in Goethe's play) Egmont's triumphant reconciliation with death emerge as *complementary;* neither tragic, nor comic interpretations of such kinetic works should completely satisfy the discerning critic. Finally, the death of Patroclus and its sequel, the long-awaited appeasement of Achilles, intimate a kind of *cosmic balance* which to reveal is the privilege of a work like the *Iliad* evoking a quasi-total world within the scope of its ecumenic tension.

4. *Beyond Genre: The Order of Literature*

These conclusions and propositions elaborate on what I believe are some of the most stimulating insights of the surveyed theories. To restate the foremost bias of the survey: I have largely ignored histories and theories of individual genres unless I could see how they might contribute to a better understanding of literature as a whole. Thus I had little chance to discuss particular generic conventions prompting writers to produce and readers to expect given types of works. This in turn meant relative neglect for certain branches of "expressive" and "pragmatic" criticism—those investigating generic conventions as reflections of historically conditioned preferences of writers and readers. (Cf. Kohler, Mantz, Pearson, Van Tieghem.) Any bias is regrettable yet some bias is unavoidable, and I am ready to defend mine. It seems to me that the better part of modern genre criticism has been more philosophical than historical or prescriptive: it has attempted to describe a few basic types of literature that *can* be written, not numerous kinds of works that *have* or, in the critic's view, *should have* been written. As a result, the finest generic classifications of our time make us look beyond their immediate concern and focus on the *order of literature,* not on *borders between literary genres.*

The same general orientation informs, I should hope, this concluding chapter. I have said next to nothing in it about such more or less strictly definable genres as Greek tragedy, Restoration comedy, the Gothic novel, or the (pseudo-) popular ballad. Nor have I been directly concerned with historical change—the central phenomenon of any literary tradition. In exchange, I have tried to indicate what can change and what remains constant in the realm of verbal art. Surely, theoretical constructs such as the thematic, dramatic, narrative, or lyric *mode of discourse,* the authorial, interpersonal, dual, or private *perspective,* the concentric, kinetic, or ecumenic *scope,* and the tragic, comic, or tragicomic *mood* are but distant pointers to the living reality of literary works. Yet they may provide a flexible conceptual framework for the historical study of more concretely definable generic traditions. And they can, I think, help explicate and evaluate any given work of imaginative literature as a presentation and representation of human action and vision.

Appendix

Free Indirect Discourse and Related Techniques[*]

It is well known that Socrates, in the third book of Plato's *Republic*, distinguished three modes of literary discourse according to whether the poet, the characters, or poet and characters alternately speak. What has been overlooked too often is this: Mindful of his interlocutor's slow understanding, Socrates illustrated his concepts of authorial, figural, and mixed speech in the manner of a "bad speaker" who "will not take the whole of the subject, but will break a piece off" in order to support his argument (392d; B. Jowett's translation). We will, of course, never know how Socrates conceived of the "whole of the subject." Yet the last twenty-three hundred years of literary history persuasively supplemented his example for mixed speech, the Homeric type of direct quotation, with new techniques of integrating *diegesis* and *mimesis*, the authorial presentation and the impersonating representation of action.[1]

* Reprinted, with permission, from *Comparative Literature*, XXIV (Winter, 1972), pp. 32–43. The original title of this paper was "Dual Perspective: Free Indirect Discourse and Related Techniques."

[1] I take the liberty of replacing "narrative," the familiar English rendering of *diegesis*, by the phrase "authorial presentation." In the context of Plato's *Republic*, the traditional translation incurs a hardly

Prose fiction is a choice example. Employing both narrative and dialogue, it has inherited the mixed status of the great epic poem, but it can also surpass the Homeric degree of structural complexity by dint of such devices as inserted poems, letters, diaries, or the presentation of a character's stream of consciousness. Beyond doubt, the original criterion of speakers must be modified if we want to adapt Plato's classification to the needs of modern criticism. Instead of asking, "Who speaks?" we should try to clarify whose perceptions, thoughts, and feelings inform the world of a given work of literature. Yet our more sophisticated line of inquiry need not dismiss Plato's early attempt at "structural" criticism. The modern critic may accept the authorial and the figural perspective as points of compass within the world of literary works, even though he questions whether the Homeric type of direct quotation is the only way in which writers interrelate those two primary modes of orientation.[2]

---

felicitous concept of drama as *that* form of narration in which mimetic representation completely supersedes narration. Furthermore, the extant fragments of rather hymnic dithyrambs do not suggest that the "pure *diegesis*" of dithyrambic poets was a narrative in our sense of the word. Indeed, the revised edition of Liddell and Scott's *Greek-English Lexicon* (1925–1940) informs us that the first recorded occurrence of the corresponding verb (*diegeomai*) should be translated as "set out in detail, describe," and that Aristotle's *Rhetoric* employs the very noun *diegesis* in the sense of "statement of the case." Thus it should be permissible to conjecture that *diegesis* meant for Plato something like "presentation"—the authorial aspect of poetry.

[2] In "Point of View in Fiction: The Development of a Critical Concept," *PMLA*, LXX (1955), Norman Friedman explicitly associated Socrates's remarks on the "three styles" of poetry with the modern concepts "telling" and "showing," widely adopted from Henry James and Percy Lubbock in recent fiction theory. In "Verbal Worlds between Action and Vision," *College English*, XXXIII (1971), I am suggesting a theory of literary discourse within a modified "Platonic" framework.

Consider, for example, the following passage from a contemporary novel, Saul Bellow's *Herzog:*

> Then the traffic opened and the cab rattled in low gear and jerked into second. "For Christ sake, let's make time," the driver said. They made a sweeping turn into Park Avenue and Herzog clutched the broken window handle. It wouldn't open. But if it opened dust would pour in. They were demolishing and raising buildings. The Avenue was filled with concrete-mixing trucks, smells of wet sand and powdery gray cement.[3]

Most readers will agree that the passage just quoted evokes a scene from Herzog's point of view, in other words, from within the stuffy cab with a broken window handle. Yet the narrator is by no means explicitly quoting Herzog's thoughts and sensations, and we might expect that he, the narrator, will emerge from the text as our only source of information. Remarkably enough, however, by the time we read the words, "But if it opened dust would pour in," we take it as a matter of course that their meaning originates in Herzog's fictive mind. How do we come to accept (and in fact hardly notice) such a radical, yet unannounced shift in perspective? Close reading of the passage will provide an answer modifying rather than contradicting the Platonic distinction between authorial and figural speech.

The first three sentences can easily be interpreted as exemplifying the Homeric type of "mixed speech": in the first and the third sentence the narrator speaks himself, and in the second he quotes one of the characters. But the fourth sentence, "It wouldn't open," defies classification in strictly Platonic terms. Observe that the pronoun 'it' refers to the window and not (as it should according to the rules of grammar) to the window *handle*. This inconsistency signals that the fourth sentence is not a natural continuation of the preceding authorial statement; the words "It wouldn't open" take their semantic departure from Herzog's intention to open the window—an intention merely implied by the narrator's statement: "Herzog clutched the broken window handle." The colloquial contracted form "wouldn't," rarely used in straight objective narration, further indicates that in a sense the narrator has yielded the floor to his character. Yet, Herzog has not become the "speaker." Were he himself to approximate the conclusion reached in his mind after the frustrated attempt to open the window, we should read: "It won't open." By substituting "wouldn't" for Herzog's "won't," the narrator assimilates figural speech to the past-tense context of authorial narration, thereby providing a smooth transition between his own perspective of the events and Herzog's which then informs the next sentence completely. Since the narrator knows, so to speak, that Herzog was unable to open the window, he could only state what would *have* happened, if the window *had* opened; the words "But if it opened dust would pour in" must be Herzog's who alone can contemplate what *would* happen if he *could* open the window. After this snatch of interior monologue, the narrator seems to resume his function as the speaker. But does he really? Standing by itself, the sixth sentence would appear, to be sure, an authorial statement. In its context, however, we tend to read the sentence "They were demolishing and raising buildings" as a retroactively provided premise for Herzog's conclusion: "if it opened dust would pour in." Thus the narrator once again substitutes his own words for Herzog's mental operations without explicitly telling the reader that he will do so. Although with the last sentence of our passage the authorial perspective regains its predominance, the figural interlude has left an important aftereffect on our minds. While "listening" to the narrator's words about concrete-mixing trucks and the smell of wet sand, we still imagine Herzog rather than the narrator or, for instance, the cab driver as the person who experiences the evoked sensory impressions. In "Qu'est-ce que la Littérature," Jean-Paul Sartre called reading "directed creation" (*création dirigée*) and argued that the examining magistrate in Dostoevsky's *Crime and Punishment* would not exist without the hatred we readers "lend" Raskolnikov toward him.[4] Turning Sartre's argument around, I submit that the broken window handle and the dusty smell of wet sand really "exist" for the reader insofar as he has become aware of Herzog's fictive sensory, emotive, and rational response to those things.

Such awareness naturally occurs while we listen to the words of a dramatic character on stage or read statements made by fictional figures rather than by a detached, omniscient narrator. Seemingly authorial sentences such as "It wouldn't open" effect similar identification with a character's perspective only because they strike us as making better sense if we assume that a mind other than the narrator's is responsible for their meaning. Since the narrator in such cases *substitutes* his words for a character's speech, thought, or sensory perception, the most adequate term suggested so far for this type of literary discourse seems to me substitutionary narration.[5] There is, of course, a good deal to be

[4] Jean-Paul Sartre, *Situations*, II (Paris, 1948), p. 95.

[5] With varying range of denotation and connotation, the term "substitutionary" has been used by John Orr in his English version of Iorgu Iordan, *An Introduction to Romance Linguistics* (London, 1937), p. 133; by Bernhard Fehr in *Aus Englands geistigen Beständen* (Frauenfeld, 1944), pp. 265ff; and by Helmut A. Hatzfeld in *A Critical Bibliography of the New Stylistics* (Chapel Hill, 1953), pp. 182ff.

said in favor of some of the other terms emerging from the extensive critical discussion of the subject: *style indirect libre, verschleierte Rede, erlebte Rede,* independent form of indirect discourse, *uneigentlich direkte Rede,* represented speech, *Rede als Tatsache, monologue intérieur indirect,* and narrated monologue.[6] Yet most critics advocating one of those rather narrow terms have focused their attention on some of the pertinent phenomena far too closely to become interested in establishing a comprehensive context for all phenomena in question. The best such context, I believe, is Plato's classification of verbal discourse, provided that we add a fourth category to the original framework. In quasi-Platonic terms this category might be described as discourse in which poet and character speak simultaneously or, more precisely, in which the narrator says *in propria persona* what one of the characters means. In such discourse, the authorial and the figural per-

[6] This is a selective list ignoring simple translations, slight variants, and overingenious coinages. The first influential employment of the quoted terms can be found in Charles Bally, "Le Style indirect libre en français moderne," *Germanisch-Romanische Monatsschrift,* IV (1912); Theodor Kalepky, "Zum 'style indirect libre' ('Verschleierte Rede')" *ibid.,* V (1913); Etienne Lorck, *Die erlebte Rede* (Heidelberg, 1921); George O. Curme, *A Grammar of the German Language* (1904), revised and enlarged ed. (New York, 1922), pp. 245ff; Gertraud Lerch, "Die uneigentlich direkte Rede," *Idealistische Neuphilologie: Festschrift für Karl Vossler* (Heidelberg, 1922); Otto Jespersen, *The Philosophy of Grammar* (London, 1924), fourth reprint (1935), pp. 291f; Eugen Lerch, "Ursprung und Bedeutung der sog. 'Erlebten Rede' ('Rede als Tatsache')," *Germanisch-Romanische Monatsschrift,* XVI (1928); Edouard Dujardin, *Le Monologue intérieur* (Paris, 1931), pp. 39f; Dorrit Cohn, "Narrated Monologue: Definition of a Fictional Style," *Comparative Literature,* XVIII (1966). For further bibliographical references cf. also Michael Gregory, "Old Bailey Speech in *A Tale of Two Cities,*" *A Review of English Literature,* VI (1965), and Werner Hoffmeister, *Studien zur erlebten Rede bei Thomas Mann and Robert Musil* (The Hague, 1965).

spective need not alternate; rather, their simultaneous presence results in a new, dual mode of vision. My following observations are intended to contribute to the exploration of the optics, as it were, of this complex perspective.

From the point of view of grammar, substitutionary narration emerges as an elliptical form of indirect quotation. Instead of saying "The defendant declared unequivocally that he was innocent," I may say: "The defendant's declaration was unequivocal; he was innocent." Much like direct quotation ("The defendant declared: 'I am innocent!' "), substitutionary narration does not reduce the most important part of the communication, namely, what the defendant said, to the status of a secondary clause introduced by 'that,' a lifeless subordinating conjunction.[7] Nevertheless, it shifts tense and grammatical person in the defendant's declaration according to the rules of indirect discourse. Thus linguists may well define substitutionary narration as a "mixture of direct and indirect speech" or "semidirect" discourse.[8] From the point of view of literary criticism, however, we do better to emphasize what separates the sentence, "The defendant's declaration was unequivocal; he was innocent," from both its direct and indirect counterpart. This separating character-

[7] French indirect discourse always depends on *si*, *qu(e)*, or an interrogative word. If "that" is dropped in English, the derivative tense employed in the quoted phrase indicates that the latter is but a secondary clause: "The defendant declared he *was* innocent." In German, the subordinating conjunction *daß* (and the transposed word order concomitant with it) need not be retained if the indirectly quoted utterance betrays its "secondary" nature by appearing in the subjunctive: *Der Angeklagte erklärte, er sei unschuldig.*

[8] Cf. A. Tobler, *Vermischte Beiträge zur französischen Grammatik*, 2. Reihe (Leipzig, 1894), pp. 132ff. and E. Legrand, *Stylistique française* (Paris, 1922).

istic is the lack of a *verbum dicendi* such as 'said,' 'asked,' 'replied,' in our case 'declared.' In direct as well as indirect discourse, such a verb would indicate that the ensuing words are part of a quotation. In the absence of a *verbum dicendi* and a subordinating conjunction, quoted speech assumes the grammatical disguise of a narrated fact—hence the adequacy of such terms as "veiled speech" (*verschleierte Rede*) and "speech as fact" (*Rede als Tatsache*) to the formal characteristics of the sentence: "The defendant's declaration was unequivocal; he was innocent."

Naturally, the veil of grammar is quickly removed from any instance of "free indirect" quotation if its meaning, style, and context signal that one mind is responsible for the form and another for the content of a statement. By the time we read of Madame Bovary, "Elle déclarait adorer les enfants; c'était sa consolation, sa joie, sa folie," [9] we know that it cannot be the narrator who tells us that Emma's little child was joy and consolation for her. Rather, reader and narrator share an ironic distance from the woman who tries to appear what she is not—a devoted mother. But through the free indirect mode of quotation the narrator may also empathize with a character's view of the fictional reality. This is very frequently the case if figural thought rather than figural speech is rendered with the dual focus of substitutionary narration. Let me illustrate this by commenting on a passage recently cited by another student of free indirect discourse.

[9] Gustave Flaubert, *Madame Bovary*, Conard edition (Paris, 1910), p. 147. In his *Style and the French Novel* (Cambridge, 1957), p. 109, Stephen Ullmann comments on this sentence: "Grammatically, 'c'était sa consolation, sa joie, sa folie' might be the author's own words, but the reader knows from the context that it is Emma, not Flaubert, who is speaking, and that she is not telling the truth."

In his *Portrait of the Artist as a Young Man,* James Joyce has his hero Stephen wait at church for confession:

The slide was shot to suddenly. The penitent came out. He was next. He stood up in terror and walked blindly into the box.

At last it had come. He knelt in the silent gloom and raised his eyes to the white crucifix suspended above him. God could see that he was sorry. He would tell all his sins. His confession would be long, long. Everybody in the chapel would know then what a sinner he had been. Let them know. It was true. But God had promised to forgive him if he was sorry. He was sorry.[10]

The latter half of his text is truly *erlebte Rede,* experienced speech. Young Stephen does not speak the words, "I will tell all my sins," but experiences them (or something like them) as they emerge from his consciousness. Instead of pressing the contents of Stephen's troubled mind into the rigid frame of verbal communication, the narrator renders them obliquely, substituting 'he' for 'I,' simple past for present, pluperfect for present perfect, and conditional for future in what would otherwise be Stephen's silent soliloquy. But this series of substitutions does not result in lack of immediacy. Repetition of emotionally charged words (sorry, long) and a brief recourse to interior monologue ("Let them know") reinforce the attentive reader's inclination to understand a sentence like "God could see that he was sorry" as Stephen's sincere conviction rather than the narrator's objective or ironic statement. Indeed, the narrator's sympathetic substitution of his

[10] James Joyce, *A Portrait of the Artist as a Young Man,* The Modern Library edition (New York, 1928), p. 165. Except for her failure to recognize the sentence "Let them know" as interior rather than "narrated" monologue, Dorrit Cohn's discussion of this passage is very illuminating (*op. cit.,* pp. 98ff.).

own words for Stephen's thoughts and feelings contributes to the esthetic illusion that we are overhearing the inner voice of an inward-turned, self-tormenting consciousness.[11]

As our texts by Flaubert, Joyce, and Bellow indicate, the applicability of the dual mode of narration ranges from substitutionary speech (such as Emma Bovary's specious declaration of love for her daughter) through substitutionary thought (such as Stephen Dedalus's preconfessional rumination) to substitutionary perception (such as Herzog's realization that the window of his cab will not open). These three cardinal colors of the full spectrum of substitutionary narration may be profitably discussed with regard to the time-honored distinction between arbitrary (conventional) and natural signs.[12]

According to a scholastic rule of thumb, while natural signs resemble what they signify, arbitrary signs do not. For the lexicographer, therefore, all but onomatopoeic words must count as arbitrary verbal signs. For the literary critic, however, not the individual words but the use to which they are

[11] In John Stuart Mill's memorable phrase, poetry makes us *overhear* "feeling confessing itself to itself" ("What is Poetry?" 1833). Interior monologues share with most lyric poems the paradox of seemingly involuntary, yet most effective verbal communication. In the next section I will discuss how substitutionary narration resolves the (often fascinating) dissonance involved in a narrator's "direct quotation" of figural thought.

[12] Jean-Baptiste DuBos's "Reflexions critiques sur la poésie et sur la peinture" (1719) is a classic treatment of this subject. Following suggestions from Jacques Maritain, *Redeeming the Time* (London, 1943), pp. 191ff., Elias Schwartz has called attention to earlier scholastic concepts in his "*Mimesis* and the Theory of Signs," *College English* (February, 1968). Cf. also W. K. Wimsatt and Cleanth Brooks, *Literary Criticism: A Short History* (New York, 1957), p. 278.

put in a specific context should provide clues as to their natural or arbitrary status. " 'For Christ sake, let's make time,' the driver said." In this sentence, quoted earlier from Bellow's *Herzog*, we can distinguish between a natural and an arbitrary mode of employing verbal signs. The words, "the driver said," are used in the "arbitrary" manner in which a statement such as "The red leaves were still on the trees" would describe a forest. In contrast, the driver's directly quoted exclamation evokes the verbal aspect of the narrated event in the "natural" way of a painted picture which, showing red leaves on trees, actually resembles what it represents. From this analysis of a sentence which Socrates would have classified as "mixed speech," two inferences can be drawn: the authorial presentation of nonverbal facts and events employs words as arbitrary, the impersonating representation of figural speech employs them as natural signs. We might add that indirectly quoted speech (for example, "The driver said that he was in a hurry") transmutes verbal events into the arbitrary mode of signification characteristic of authorial discourse.[13]

Yet the contradistinction between verbal and nonverbal components of the worlds that literary works evoke is by no means exhaustive. A considerable portion of such imaginative worlds consists of mental events in the characters' minds, and I submit that those events constitute a third distinct realm of

[13] My opinion that directly quoted figural speech relies on the "natural" mode of signification is anticipated in G. E. Lessing's letter of May 26, 1769, to Friedrich Nicolai: ". . . die höchste Gattung der Poesie ist die, welche die willkürlichen Zeichen gänzlich zu natürlichen macht. Das aber ist die dramatische: denn in dieser hören die Worte auf, willkürliche Zeichen zu sein und werden natürliche Zeichen willkürlicher Dinge." Cf. René Wellek, *A History of Modern Criticism*, Vol. 1 (New Haven, 1955), pp. 164 f.

mimesis. We may call this realm *quasi-verbal* for the following reason. While mental events (whether rational, emotive,
volitive, or sensory) are not strictly verbal, no articulate
account can be given of them, not even to the mind in which
they occur, save by means of words. Thus whenever a person
is fully conscious of his mental operations, something related
to, yet different from, verbal communication can be assumed
as present in his mind, and the possibility of giving detailed
verbal accounts of dreams and hallucinations suggests that
even subconscious mental processes involve quasi-verbal
operations in human minds. Having thus distinguished mental
events as quasi-verbal from both the verbal and the nonverbal contents of literary works, we can better understand
why substitutionary narration provides a singularly adequate
mode of evoking whatever goes on in a character's mind.
Compare, in this respect, the dual mode of signification to the
function of verbal signs in exclusively authorial and exclusively figural discourse. On the one hand, the "arbitrary"
signs of authorial narration treat mental operations as though
they were altogether nonverbal—hence the static, often lifeless quality in much "internal analysis" of figural thought
by omniscient narrators.[14] On the other hand, the "natural"
or rather *pseudonatural* signs making up a silent soliloquy
fully verbalize the quasi-verbal contents of a character's
mind, thereby treating figural thought as though it were
figural speech—another fundamental distortion which is
mitigated rather than removed by devices suggestive of "free
association" in otherwise speechlike interior monologues.
Witness, by contrast, the subtle manner of rendering figural

[14] "Internal analysis" is Lawrence E. Bowling's term for the authorial summary of mental events. Cf. his "What Is the Stream of
Consciousness Technique?" PMLA LXV (1950).

thought in our passage from *A Portrait*. Not allowing Stephen "to speak for himself," Joyce avoids having to assert that the boy explicitly thought "God has promised to forgive me if I am sorry"—no one thinks quite so explicitly. At the same time, the writer also avoids rendering figural thought from a narrator's external perspective and analytical distance. Instead of employing words as pseudonatural or arbitrary signs, Joyce evokes Stephen's quasi-verbal inner struggle for faith and mental balance in the dual mode of *pseudoarbitrary* signification. He prefers intimating to analyzing or verbalizing what cannot be analyzed or verbalized completely: psychic life.

Let us return to Herzog's quasi-verbal perception of the nonverbal fact that the window of the cab "won't open." Had Herzog said something to the driver about the window, the words in quotation marks could have served as natural signs of his verbal utterance. In order to convey an *unexpressed* sense of frustration, so typical of Herzog's introspective character, Bellow of course preferred the substitutionary "wouldn't" to both its authorial and its figural homologue. The authorial statement, "The window did not open," would have consisted of arbitrary signs, best suited to refer to nonverbal facts. The figural phrase, "It won't open," would have suggested through its natural mode of signification that Herzog gave verbal expression to a conscious observation. Only Bellow's "It wouldn't open" with its dual perspective could succeed in approximating the quasi-verbal nature of Herzog's given cursory perception.

Substitutionary speech is different. Flaubert surely did not try to approximate the verbal nature of Madame Bovary's statement about children when he decided to render her words in the oblique mode of substitutionary narration. Such approximation would indeed be effected by quoting Emma's utterance directly: "Elle déclarait: 'J'adore les enfants. C'est ma consolation, ma joie, ma folie.'" On the contrary, Flaubert preferred the pseudoarbitrary to the natural mode of signification in order to divest Emma's utterance of its straightforward directness—a quality "undeserved" by the objectively false statement. In other words, Flaubert's use of substitutionary speech throws Emma's subconscious lie, the tragicomedy of her self-deception, into high relief. But the question remains: Whose unformulated skepticism as to Emma's ultimate sincerity finds its subtle expression in the substitutionary phrase, "c'était sa consolation, sa joie, sa folie"? Her interlocutors', perhaps. More significantly, however, that phrase in its ironic context points to the omnipresent yet invisible creator of Emma's world—the author who refuses to verbalize his obvious yet unobtrusive, indeed quasi-verbal attitude towards his creature.[15]

Writers have employed the dual perspective even before La Fontaine said of that worrisome *nouveau riche*, the cobbler Grégoire: "Si quelque chat faisait du bruit/Le chat prenait l'argent."[16] Yet, in the literature of the last hundred years or so, substitutionary narration has assumed exceptional impor-

[15] Cf. the famous letter of December 9, 1852, in which Flaubert postulates that "L'auteur, dans son oeuvre, doit être comme Dieu dans l'univers, présent partout et visible nulle part." It is surely no accident that the employment of the dual perspective became almost commonplace with Flaubert and other detached, ostensibly impersonal novelists. Unaware of the first French and German articles on substitutionary narration, Percy Lubbock brilliantly circumscribed both its ironic and empathic function in *Madame Bovary* and Henry James's *The Ambassadors;* cf. *The Craft of Fiction* (London, 1921), *passim.*

[16] "Le Savetier et le financier" from the eighth book of *Fables.* Cf. Albert Thibaudet, *Gustave Flaubert* (Paris, 1922), p. 281.

tance. In view of this development, propelled by growing interest in uneditorialized figural consciousness, certain basic precepts of literary criticism invite reconsideration. Take for instance, Aristotle's dictum in Chapter 24 of the *Poetics:* "The poet should say very little *in propria persona,* as he is no imitator when doing that" (1460a; I. Bywater's translation). In the light of Plato's threefold classification of literary discourse, this principle has often been unconditionally accepted or rejected. But the charge of not being imitative, that is, of not representing human beings, cannot be leveled against substitutionary speech, thought, and perception. These dual modes of discourse may consist of seemingly authorial statements, yet they clearly evoke a character's sensory or mental vision, sometimes even stylistic peculiarities of his speech. Furthermore, substitutionary narration is not the only narrative method in which the dual perspective prevails. Figural perspective permeates authorial narration in what might be called *represented perception* as well.[17] Consider the following sentence: "Peter saw the car disappear in the distance." Although the speaker of this sentence functions as our only apparent source of information, he does not mean to say that the car Peter saw disappearing actually disappeared; the statement points to a mind other than the speaker's as responsible for the meaning of the word "disappear." Much like our previous instances of substitutionary narration, represented perception involves the double focus of authorial and figural perspective. It corroborates, therefore, the evidence that certain narrative passages in which the characters do not actually speak meet Aristotle's demand of mimetic representation provided that we replace his Pla-

[17] Cf. Anna G. Hatcher, *"Voir* as a Modern Novelistic Device," *Philological Quarterly,* XXIII (1944).

tonic criterion of figural speech by the more inclusive one of figural point of view.

Similar reconsideration may reveal the solid core of the central argument in Gotthold Ephraim Lessing's *Laokoon*.[18] According to Lessing's advice, the writer must seek to establish a "convenient relationship" (*bequemes Verhältnis*) between the temporal progress and the subject matter of his discourse. Rather than try (and fail) to depict *spatial objects* with a painter's meticulous concern for detail, Lessing's ideal poet concentrates on delineating *temporal events;* much as Homer makes us imagine Helen's beauty by telling us about the effect of her looks on the old men of Troy, the literary artist is advised to prefer narrated action to pseudopictorial description. Beyond doubt, Lessing's remarks point to a rather natural way of temporalizing otherwise static objects. As our previous examples for substitutionary and represented perception indicate, the writer may evoke any part of his imaginative world through the response it elicits from a fictive consciousness. If you say "The Johnsons' red brick house was large," you describe an object in space without reference to concrete time. But if you say "Peter caught sight of the Johnsons' red brick house," you report a mental event occurring at one particular moment of actual or imagined time. Even partially negative statements like "Peter did not notice in the dark how large the Johnsons' house was" convey their information as suggestive of a definite temporal context, while no such context is implied by the sequence of words in our original sentence: "The Johnsons' red brick house was large." In contrast to pure description, represented perception refers to some action, however rudimentary; and the "action" of Peter's noticing or not noticing the color or the

18 Cf. esp. Chapter 16.

size of the Johnsons' house evokes a human being with the temporal dimension of his existence in the listener's or reader's mind.

The same holds for substitutionary perception. In the Saul Bellow passage quoted at the beginning of this paper, we are made to witness psychic action—Herzog's momentary frustration about the broken window handle and his ensuing realization that even if he could open the window, only dust and no fresh air would pour in. At the same time we are less prompted to visualize objects—the dust or the window handle—which might distract from what literature can best represent: human beings in action. Of course, modern authors often temporalize spatial objects in a way Lessing is not likely to have foreseen. Homer narrates how the elders of Troy discuss Helen's beauty, how Hephaistos embellishes the shield of Achilles: such are Lessing's models for the poetic procedure he advocates. Bellow's method is different. Instead of the intersubjective time involved in a conversation or in the divine smith's action, the immeasurable flux of internal time, Bergson's *durée*, is implied by the evocation of the dust of Park Avenue as something Herzog prefers not to breath in.[19] Yet substitutionary and represented perception as well as substitutionary speech and thought evoke *durée* without unduly separating it from the public dimension of *temps*. Henri Bergson's theory of private duration as the only form of genuine human temporality finds its literary parallel in interior monologues with their exclusively figural rendering of consciousness. The dual modes of evoking mental events in turn affirm both the private and the public relevance of time: substitutionary narration and related techniques embed fig-

[19] Cf. Shiv K. Kumar, *Bergson and the Stream of Consciousness Novel* (New York, 1963).

ural *durée* in the narrative context of time's intersubjective progress. Abandoning the visual metaphor of perspective, one might say that the dual modes of narration make the ticking of each character's private time audible as one voice in the temporal polyphony of his world.

Having ventured into areas of investigation that connect literary criticism with philosophy, I would like to add a final word on an epistemological aspect of the dual perspective. Any verbal statement involves the principle of selection, since many more statements could be made about the same thing, and many other things could become the subject matter of discourse. This state of affairs is more or less plausibly hidden behind authorial statements of omniscient narrators. "Everything was in confusion in the Oblonsky household. The wife had found out that the husband had had an affair with their French governess and had told him that she could not go on living in the same house with him." Since the narrator of such a passage, taken from the first chapter of Tolstoy's *Anna Karenina*, pretends to know everything about everything, his discourse appears to deal with actual "things" rather than certain "facts" which, on specific occasions, may become manifest about those things to a mind. In contrast, passages employing the dual perspective intimate that a selection of facts has ben carried out by a human consciousness. An example: "Peter turned around. His sister had put on their mother's wedding dress!" Having turned around, Peter surely sees other things too, but the narrator employing the dual perspective merely tells us about the fact that "registers" in Peter's consciousness. In this manner, a good deal of modern fiction parallels the highly selective functioning of human minds. Of course, no creative writer needs to decide whether the world consists of *things* or, as Wittgenstein argued, *facts*.[20] Yet, verbal discourse in which authorial and figural perspectives interact tends to suggest that an objective universe of things may be approached through our subjective awareness of selected facts about it.

[20] Ludwig Wittgenstein, *Tractatus Logico-Philosophicus* (1918), i.i: "The world is the totality of facts, not of things."

References[*]

Abrams, Meyer H. *The Mirror and the Lamp*. Paperback ed. New York, 1958. Pp. 6–29.

Adorno, Theodor W. "Über epische Naivetät" (1943); "Der Standort des Erzählers im zeitgenössischen Roman (1954); "Rede über Lyrik und Gesellschaft" (1957). In *Noten zur Literatur*, Vol. I. Frankfort, 1958.

Aristotle. "Nicomachean Ethics," trans. W. D. Ross; "Poetics," trans. Ingram Bywater. In *Introduction to Aristotle*, Richard McKeon, ed. New York, 1947.

Barber, C. L. *Shakespeare's Festive Comedy*. Princeton, 1959.

Barthes, Roland. *Le Degré zéro de l'écriture*. Paris, 1953.

Behrens, Irene. *Die Lehre von der Einteilung der Dichtkunst*. Halle, 1940.

Bentley, Eric. *The Life of the Drama*. New York, 1964.

Bergson, Henri. *Le Rire*. Paris, 1900.

Beriger, Leonhard. *Die literarische Wertung*. Halle, 1934.

Boeckh, Joachim G. "Literaturforschung vor neuen Aufgaben," *Neue Deutsche Literatur*, IV (August, 1956), pp. 125–32.

Bonnet, Henri. *Roman et poésie*. Paris, 1951.

Booth, Wayne C. *The Rhetoric of Fiction*. Chicago, 1961.

Bovet, Ernest. *Lyrisme, épopée, drame*. Paris, 1911.

[*] This is a list of works quoted in the book exclusive of the Appendix. Whenever page numbers could not be conveniently supplied in the text, the information appears in the appropriate entry as, for instance, in the Friedrich Schlegel references below.

Brooks, Cleanth. "The Language of Paradox." In *The Well-Wrought Urn*. New York, 1947.

——. *Literary Criticism*. See Wimsatt, W. K., and C. Brooks.

Brunetière, Ferdinand. *L'Évolution des genres dans l'histoire de la littérature*. Paris, 1890.

Bruno, Giordano. *Eroici furori*. Paris, 1585.

Burke, Kenneth. *Attitudes toward History*. Paperback ed. Boston, 1961.

——. *The Philosophy of Literary Form*. Paperback ed. New York, 1957.

Cassirer, Ernst. *Philosophie der symbolischen Formen. Erster Teil: Die Sprache*. Berlin, 1923.

Chaucer, Geoffrey. *Canterbury Tales*. W. W. Skeat, ed. New York, 1929. P. 236: the Monk's Tale on the "manner of Tragedie."

Cook, Albert. *The Dark Voyage and the Golden Mean*. Cambridge, Mass., 1949.

Crane, Ronald S., ed. *Critics and Criticism*. Chicago, 1952. Includes essays by R. S. Crane ("The Concept of Plot and the Plot of *Tom Jones*," 1950) and Elder Olson ("An Outline of Poetic Theory," 1949; "William Empson, Contemporary Criticism, and Poetic Diction," 1950; "A Dialogue on Symbolism," 1952).

Croce, Benedetto. *Aesthetic*, trans. D. Ainslie. London, 1922.

——. *Problemi di estetica*. Bari, 1910. P. 111: on the "eternal war" he swore to wage against generic divisions.

Daiches, David. *Critical Approaches to Literature*. New Jersey, 1956.

Diderot, Denis. "Discours sur la poésie dramatique." In *Oeuvres*, A. Billy, ed. Paris, 1946. Pp. 1310f: on the ideal critic.

Dohrn, Wolf. *Die künstlerische Darstellung als Problem der Aesthetik*. Hamburg and Leipzig, 1907.

Ehrenpreis, Irwin. *The "Types Approach" to Literature*. New York, 1945.

Eliot, Thomas Stearns. "Hamlet and his Problems" (1919). In

Selected Essays. New York, 1932. Pp. 124f: on the "objective correlative."

——. *The Three Voices of Poetry.* New York, 1954.

Ellis-Fermor, Una. *The Frontiers of Drama.* 2nd ed. London, 1964.

Elster, Ernst. *Über die Elemente der Poesie und den Begriff des Dramatischen.* Marburg, 1903.

Empson, William. *Seven Types of Ambiguity.* London, 1930.

Erlich, Victor. *Russian Formalism.* The Hague, 1955.

Fergusson, Francis. *The Idea of a Theater.* Paperback ed. Garden City, 1954. P. 251: on "histrionic sensibility."

Fernandez, Ramon. "La Méthode de Balzac." In *Messages.* Paris, 1926.

Fielding, Henry. *Joseph Andrews.* London, 1742. Preface: "a comic romance is a comic epic-poem in prose."

——. *Tom Jones.* London, 1749. Book 2, Chapter 1: contrast between "extraordinary scene" and the "unobserved" periods of fictive time.

Fischer, Ernst. "Das Endspiel und Iwan Denissowitsch." In *Kunst und Koexistenz.* Hamburg, 1966.

Flemming, Willi. "Das Problem von Dichtungsgattung und -art," *Studium Generale,* XII (1959), pp. 38–60.

Fletcher, Angus. See Krieger, M., ed.

Fracastoro, Hieronymus. "Naugerius, sive de poetica dialogus." In *Opera omnia philosophica et medica.* Venice, 1555.

Friedemann, Käte. *Die Rolle des Erzählers in der Epik.* Leipzig, 1910.

Friedman, Melvin. *Stream of Consciousness.* New Haven, 1955. Pp. 3, 18ff, 262: on "poetry" in the modern novel.

Friedman, Norman. "Point of View in Fiction," PMLA, LXX (1955), pp. 1160–1184.

Frye, Northrop. *Anatomy of Criticism.* Princeton, 1957.

——. "The Archetypes of Literature" (1951). In *Fables of Identity.* New York, 1963. P. 16: on the "natural cycle."

——. "The Developing Imagination." In *Learning in Language and Literature*. Cambridge, Mass., 1963.

——. *A Natural Perspective: The Development of Shakespearean Comedy and Romance*. New York, 1965.

——. *The Well-Tempered Critic*. Bloomington, 1963.

Goethe, Johann Wolfgang. *Gedenkausgabe der Werke, Briefe und Gespräche*. E. Beutler, ed. Zürich, 1948. XX, 472: epistolary novels are dramatic (letter of December 23, 1797, to Friedrich Schiller).

——. *Sämtliche Werke*. E. von der Hellen, ed. Stuttgart, 1902–1912. V, 223: on the three "natural forms of poetry" (*Noten und Abhandlungen zu besserem Verständnis des West-Östlichen Divans.* 1819); XVIII, 34: epic "events" *versus* dramatic "deeds" (*Wilhelm Meisters Lehrjahre*. Book 5, Chapter 7. 1796); XXIV, 225: an unheard-of event as proper subject matter for a *Novelle* (Conversation with Eckermann on January 25, 1827); XXXVI, 149ff: contrast between detached rhapsodist and involved actor ("Über epische und dramatische Dichtung von Goethe und Schiller," 1797); XXXVIII, 161f: on Molière's *Misanthrope* (an 1828 book review in *Über Kunst und Altertum*, Vol. 6).

Greene, Thomas M. *The Descent from Heaven*. New Haven, 1963.

Gregory, Michael. "Old Bailey Speech in *A Tale of Two Cities*," *A Review of English Literature*, VI (1965), pp. 42–55.

Guérard, Albert. *Preface to World Literature*. New York, 1940.

Guillén, Claudio. "Poetics as System," *Comparative Literature*, XXII (1970), pp. 193–222.

Guthke, Karl S. *Modern Tragicomedy*. New York, 1966.

Hamburger, Käte. *Die Logik der Dichtung*. Stuttgart, 1957.

——. "Zum Strukturproblem der epischen und der dramatischen Dichtung," *Deutsche Vierteljahrsschrift für Literaturwissenschaft und Geistesgeschichte*, XXV (1951), pp. 1–26.

Hartl, Robert. *Versuch einer psychologischen Grundlegung der Dichtungsgattungen*. Vienna, 1924.

Hartman, Geoffrey H.   "Ghostlier Demarcations." See Krieger, M., ed.

Hegel, Georg Wilhelm Friedrich.   *Ästhetik*. Berlin and Weimar, 1965. II, 424 and 448: association of the epic with occurrence, drama with action; II, 450: the "total world" of the epic; II, 512f: about objective epic, subjective lyric, and their synthesis in drama; II, 517 and 521: colliding substantial forces, the unity of "total movement" in tragic drama; II, 552f: contrast between comedy and tragedy.

Heidegger, Martin.   *Sein und Zeit*. Halle, 1927. Pp. 336, 340, 346.

Herder, Johann Gottfried.   *Sämtliche Werke*. B. Suphan, ed. Berlin, 1877–1913. XVIII, 138: against generic classifications; XXVII, 171 and XXXII, 62: about lyric poetry.

Hernadi, Paul.   "Dual Perspective: Free Indirect Discourse and Related Techniques," *Comparative Literature*, XXIV (Winter 1972), pp. 32–43.

——.   "Verbal Worlds between Action and Vision." *College English*, XXXIII (1971), pp. 18–31.

Hirsch, Eric Donald.   *Validity in Interpretation*. New Haven, 1967.

Hirt, Ernst.   *Das Formgesetz der epischen, dramatischen und lyrischen Dichtung*. Leipzig und Berlin, 1923.

Hugo, Victor.   Preface to *Cromwell* (1827). In *Théatre complet*. Paris, 1963. I, 410ff.

Humboldt, Wilhelm von.   *Über Goethes Hermann und Dorothea* (1799). In *Werke*, E. Leitzmann, ed. Vol. 2. Berlin, 1904. P. 228: on epic poetry.

Humphrey, Robert.   *Stream of Consciousness in the Modern Novel*. Berkeley, 1954. Pp. 73 and 121: on "poetic" devices in the novel.

Ingarden, Roman.   *Das literarische Kunstwerk*. 3rd rev. ed. Tübingen, 1965.

Jakobson, Roman.   "Randbemerkungen zur Prosa des Dichters Pasternak," *Slavische Rundschau*, VII (1935), pp. 357–373.

James, Henry. *The Art of the Novel: Critical Prefaces*. R. P. Blackmur, ed. New York, 1934. P. 5.

Jean Paul. See Richter, Jean Paul Friedrich.

Jekels, Ludwig. *Selected Papers*. New York, 1952.

Jolles, André. *Einfache Formen: Legende, Sage, Mythe, Rätsel, Spruch, Kasus, Memorabile, Märchen, Witz*. 2nd rev. ed. Halle, 1956.

Jones, Sir William. "Essay on the Arts Commonly Called Imitative." In *Poems Consisting Chiefly of Translations from the Asiatick Languages*. London, 1772.

Joyce, James. *A Portrait of the Artist as a Young Man*. London, 1916.

Kayser, Wolfgang. *Das sprachliche Kunstwerk*. 6th rev. ed. Bern, 1960.

Klaus, Carl H. See Scholes, Robert, and Carl H. Klaus.

Kleiner, Juliusz. "The Role of Time in Literary Genres," *Zagadnienia Rodzajów Literackich*, II (1959), pp. 5–12.

Klotz, Volker. *Geschlossene und offene Form im Drama*. 2nd ed. Munich, 1962.

Knights, L. C. *How Many Children Had Lady Macbeth?* Cambridge, 1933.

Köhler, Wolfgang. *Gestalt Psychology*. New York, 1929.

Kohler, Pierre. "Contribution à une philosophie des genres," *Helicon*, I (1938), pp. 233–244; II (1940), pp. 135–147.

Krieger, Murray, ed. *Northrop Frye in Modern Criticism*. New York, 1966.

Langer, Susanne K. *Feeling and Form*. New York, 1953.

——. *Philosophy in a New Key*. Sixth paperback ed. New York, 1954.

Lessing, Gotthold Ephraim. *Sämtliche Schriften*. K. Lachmann and F. Muncker, eds. Stuttgart, 1886–1924. X, 82f: on tragicomedy (*Hamburgische Dramaturgie*, 70. Stück).

Lévi-Strauss, Claude. "Les Limites de la notion de structure en ethnologie." In *Sens et usages du terme structure dans les sciences humaines et sociales*, R. Bastide, ed. The Hague, 1962.

Longinus. "On Literary Excellence." In *Literary Criticism: From Plato to Dryden*, A. H. Gilbert, ed. New York, 1940. Chapter 17.

Lubbock, Percy. *The Craft of Fiction*. Sixth reprint. London, 1939.

Ludwig, Otto. "Formen der Erzählung." In *Gesammelte Schriften*, A. Stern, ed. Leipzig, 1891. Vol. VI.

Lukács, Georg. *Die Eigenart des Ästhetischen*. In *Werke*. Vols. XI and XII. Neuwied, 1963.

———. "Erzählen oder Beschreiben?" (1936). In *Probleme des Realismus*. Berlin, 1955.

———. "Faust-Studien" (1940). In *Werke*. Vol. VI. Neuwied, 1965.

———. "Gedanken zu einer Ästhetik des Kinos" (1913). In *Schriften zur Literatursoziologie*, P. Lutz, ed. 2nd ed. Neuwied, 1963.

———. "Gottfried Keller" (1939). In *Werke*. Vol. VII. Neuwied, 1964.

———. *Der historische Roman* (1937). In *Werke*. Vol. VI. Neuwied, 1965.

———. *History of the Development of Modern Drama*. (In Hungarian: Budapest, 1911.) Quoted here from the German version of the Introduction "Zur Soziologie des modernen Dramas," *Archiv für Sozialwissenschaft und Sozialpolitik*, XXXVIII (1914), pp. 303–345 and 662–706.

———. "Minna von Barnhelm" (1963). In *Werke*. Vol. VII. Neuwied, 1964.

———. "Puschkins Platz in der Weltliteratur" (1949). In *Werke*. Vol. V. Neuwied, 1964.

———. "Reichtum, Chaos, und Form" (1909). See *Die Seele und die Formen*.

———. *Die Seele und die Formen*. Berlin, 1911.

———. "Solschenizyn: Ein Tag im Leben des Iwan Denissowitsch" (1964). In *Werke*. Vol. V. Neuwied, 1964.

———. *Die Theorie des Romans* (1916). 3rd ed. Neuwied, 1963.

———. *Wider den mißverstandenen Realismus*. Hamburg, 1957.

Mantz, Harold Elmer. "Types in Literature," *Modern Language Review*, XII (1917), pp. 469–479.

Meyer, Theodor A. *Das Stilgesetz der Poesie*. Leipzig, 1901.

Mill, John Stuart. "What Is Poetry?" (1833). In *Dissertations and Discussions*. 2nd ed. London, 1867. I, 71f: on "soliloquy overheard."

Müller, Günther. "Bemerkungen zur Gattungspoetik," *Philosophischer Anzeiger*, III (1928), pp. 129–147.

Myers, Henry Alonzo. *Tragedy: A View of Life*. Ithaca, 1956.

Novalis (Friedrich von Hardenberg). "Neue Fragmentensammlungen" (1798). In *Schriften*, P. Kluckhohn, ed. Leipzig, 1928. II, 328, 348, 352, 359, 374: on lyric, epic, and dramatic literature.

Olson, Elder. *The Theory of Comedy*. Bloomington, 1968.

——. *Tragedy and the Theory of Drama*. Detroit, 1961.

——. See Crane, R. S., ed.

Pearson, Norman H. "Literary Forms and Types," *The English Institute Annual, 1940*, New York, 1941. Pp. 61–72.

Petersen, Julius. *Die Wissenschaft von der Dichtung*. Berlin, 1939.

Petsch, Robert. *Die lyrische Dichtung*. Halle, 1939.

——. *Wesen und Formen des Dramas*. Halle, 1945.

——. *Wesen und Formen der Erzählkunst*. Halle, 1934.

Plato. *The Republic*. Trans. B. Jowett. Oxford, 1898.

Popper, Karl R. *The Logic of Scientific Discovery*. London, 1959.

Richardson, Samuel. Postscript to *Clarissa* (1747–48). Stratford, 1930. VIII, 309: "the History (or rather Dramatic Narrative) of Clarissa."

Richter, Jean Paul Friedrich. *Vorschule der Ästhetik*. Norbert Miller, ed. Munich, 1963. P. 237: drama is more objective than the epic poem; p. 272: epic "occurrence" *versus* dramatic "action" and the association of the lyric with the present, the epic with the past, and drama with the future.

Rousseau, Jean-Jacques. *Lettre à M. D'Alembert*. Amsterdam, 1758. P. 55: on Molière's *Misanthrope*.

Ruttkowski, Wolfgang Victor. *Die literarischen Gattungen.* Bern, 1968.

Sartre, Jean-Paul. *Situations.* Vol. I. Paris, 1947. Includes 1938 and 1939 reviews of novels by Dos Passos, Faulkner, Mauriac, and Blanchot.

——. *Situations.* Vol. II. Paris, 1948. Contains *Qu'est-ce que la Littérature?*

Schelling, Friedrich Wilhelm Joseph. *Sämtliche Werke.* Stuttgart, 1856–61. V, 639ff: about objectivity and subjectivity of genres ("Philosophie der Kunst," 1802–1803).

Schlegel, August Wilhelm. *Vorlesungen über schöne Literatur und Kunst.* J. Minor, ed. Stuttgart, 1884. I, 357: about objective epic, subjective lyric, and their synthesis in drama.

Schlegel, Friedrich. *Kritische Schriften.* Wolfdietrich Rasch, ed. Munich, 1958. P. 30 about systems from *Das Athenaeum* (1798–1800); p. 325: about the conceptual unity of novels ("Gespräch über die Poesie," 1799).

——. *Literary Notebooks.* H. Eichner, ed. Toronto, 1957. Pp. 48 and 204: on subjective lyric, objective drama, and their epic synthesis; p. 175: subjective lyric, objective epic, "objective-subjective" drama.

Scholes, Robert. *Elements of Fiction.* New York, 1968.

——. *Elements of Poetry.* New York, 1969.

——, and Carl H. Klaus. *Elements of Drama.* New York, 1971.

——, and Carl H. Klaus. *Elements of the Essay.* New York, 1969.

Schopenhauer, Arthur. *Die Welt als Wille und Vorstellung.* 4th extended ed. Leipzig, 1873. II, 493f: "synthetic" position of the epic between subjective lyric and objective drama.

Scott, Walter. Self-review of *Tales of My Landlord* (1817). In *The Miscellaneous Prose Works.* Vol. XIX. Edinburgh, 1835. Pp. 2ff: contrast between "the common language of narrative" and the "dramatic shape" of scenic narration.

Seidler, Herbert. *Die Dichtung.* 2nd ed. Stuttgart, 1965.

Sengle, Friedrich. *Die literarische Formenlehre.* Stuttgart, 1967.

Spitzer, Leo. "Über zeitliche Perspektive in der neueren französischen Lyrik," *Die Neueren Sprachen*, XXXI (1923), pp. 241–266.

Spoerri, Theophil. *Präludium zur Poesie.* Berlin, 1929.

Staiger, Emil. *Grundbegriffe der Poetik.* 6th extended ed. Zurich, 1963.

——. "Time and the Poetic Imagination," *Times Literary Supplement*, September 27, 1963. Reprinted in *The Critical Moment*, London, 1964.

Stanzel, Franz K. *Die typischen Erzählsituationen im Roman*, Vienna, 1955.

Stöhr, Adolf. *Psychologie.* Revised ed. Vienna, 1922. P. 354.

Szondi, Peter. *Theorie des modernen Dramas.* 2nd ed. Frankfort, 1959.

Tynjanov, Yurij. See Erlich, Victor. *Russian Formalism.*

Van Tieghem, Paul. "La Question des genres littéraires," *Helicon*, I (1938), pp. 95–101.

Viëtor, Karl. "Probleme der literarischen Gattungsgeschichte," *Deutsche Vierteljahrsschrift für Literaturwissenschaft und Geistesgeschichte*, IX (1931), pp. 425–447.

Vischer, Friedrich Theodor. *Ästhetik.* Stuttgart, 1846–1857. V, 1260: association of the lyric with the present, the epic with the past, and drama with the future.

Vivas, Eliseo. "Literary Classes: Some Problems," *Genre*, I (1968), pp. 97–105.

Walpole, Horace. Letter of August 16, 1776, to the Countess of Upper Ossory: on tragedy and comedy. *The Letters of Horace Walpole.* Mrs. Paget Toynbee, ed. Oxford, 1903–1905. IX, 403.

Walzel, Oskar. "Schicksale des lyrischen Ichs" (1916). In *Das Wortkunstwerk.* Leipzig, 1926.

Warren, Robert Penn. "Pure and Impure Poetry," (1942). In *Critiques and Essays in Criticism*, R. W. Stallman, ed. New York, 1949.

Weber, Max. "Die 'Objektivität' sozialwissenschaftlicher und sozialpolitischer Erkenntnis" (1904). In *Gesammelte Aufsätze zur Wissenschaftslehre*. Tübingen, 1951. Pp. 190f: on "ideal types."

Wellek, René. "Genre Theory, the Lyric, and 'Erlebnis'" (1967). In *Discriminations*. New Haven, 1970.

Whitmore, Charles E. "The Validity of Literary Definitions," PMLA, XXXIX (1924), pp. 722–736.

Wimsatt, William K. "Criticism as Myth." See Krieger, M., ed.

——, and Monroe C. Beardsley. *The Verbal Icon*. Lexington, 1954.

——, and Cleanth Brooks. *Literary Criticism: A Short History*. New York, 1957.

Wordsworth, Williams. Preface to the 2nd ed. (1800) of his and Coleridge's *Lyrical Ballads:* on the "spontaneous overflow of powerful feelings . . . recollected in tranquillity."

Wundt, Max. "Literaturwissenschaft und Weltanschauungslehre." In *Philosophie der Literaturwissenschaft*, E. Ermatinger, ed. Berlin, 1930.

Index

BEYOND GENRE

Designed by R. E. Rosenbaum.
Composed by Vail-Ballou Press, Inc.,
in 11 point linotype Janson, 3 points leaded,
with display lines in monotype Deepdene.
Printed letterpress from type by Vail-Ballou Press
on Warren's No. 66 text, 60 pound basis.
with the Cornell University Press watermark.
Bound by Vail-Ballou Press
in Columbia book cloth
and stamped in All Purpose foil.

Library of Congress Cataloging in Publication Data
(For library cataloging purposes only)

Hernadi, Paul, date.
  Beyond genre.

  Bibliography: p.
  1. Criticism. 2. Literary form. I. Title.
PN81.H4   801'.95   72-4175
ISBN 0-8014-0732-X